Blood on the Hills

by Earl B. Pilgrim

Earl B Pilgrim

Blood on the Hills

Earl B. Pilgrim

Flanker Press Ltd.
St. John's, Newfoundland
2000

Edited by Burton K. Janes, Eileen Riche.
Design and layout by City Design

Published by Flanker Press Ltd.
P O Box 2522, Stn C., St. John's, Newfoundland
Canada A1C 6K1 (709) 739-4477
email: info@flankerpress.com
Website: www.flankerpress.com

Printed in Canada by
Robinson-Blackmore Printing and Publishing Limited

Canadian Cataloguing in Publication Data

Pilgrim, Earl B. (Earl Baxter), 1939-

Blood on the hills

ISBN 1-894463-07-2

1. Pilgrim, Earl B. (Earl Baxter), 1939- .2. Poaching --
Newfoundland. ..3. Game protection -- Newfoundland
I. Title.   SK471.N48P55 2000
333.95'4916'09718 ...C00-950140-1

This book is dedicated to the late John Penny (Broadcaster).

John was a special friend of wildlife and of the officers who went beyond the call of duty. As a broadcaster, he always gave wildlife conservation a high profile and gave each officer his due. The voice of John Penny called many people in western Newfoundland through CBC radio, Corner Brook; so much so that his voice still seems to ring through the Humber Valley and the Great Northern Peninsula.

John passed away a few years ago, and we all miss him.

ACKNOWLEDGEMENTS

Without the help of the following people, this true story would not have been written: my wife Beatrice (Compton) Pilgrim, who with patience helped put the book together; my daughter Nadine, who did typing at the Newfoundland Career Academy; Mr. David Smallwood; Mr. Duane Gordon; Lisa Sheehan; Marlene Laing; Eric Kinden; Norman Muise; Peter St.Croix; Robert Whitten; Vincent Porter; Winston Anstey; James Maloney; Baine Pilgrim; Howard Lavers; Nish Dobbin; Norman Muise Jr.; Calvin Bartin; Robert Penton; Hayward White; Dr. Reg Ryan and my co-worker, Raymond Norman.

Special thanks to James Hancock, Hon. Chuck Furey, Kay Mullins, Clarence Maloney, Randy Trask, Junior Canning, Sam Compton, Don Gillard, Ross Decker, Gayle Randell, Glenda Cull, Freeman Cull, Edward Pilgrim, Ivan Manuel, Ross Compton, Ford Hancock Sr., Prem Applin, George Humby, Rex Boyd, Bob Way, the late Oliver Fillier, Fred Newman, Ray Fillier, Len Wilcox, Naomi Wilcox, Carl Pilgrim and Dr. Elke Dettmer.

The publisher wishes to thank Jerry Cranford, Margo Cranford, Vera McDonald, and Eileen Riche.

ABOUT THE AUTHOR

Earl B. Pilgrim (John Christian) was born in St. Anthony in 1939. He received his early education in Roddickton, later studying Forestry at the College of Trades and Technology in St. John's.

He began his adult career in 1960 as an Infantryman in the Canadian Army, serving with the Princess Patricia's Canadian Light Infantry. While there, he became involved in the sport of boxing, eventually becoming the Canadian Light Heavyweight Boxing Champion.

Following a stint in the Forces, he took a job as a Forest Ranger with the Newfoundland and Labrador Forestry Department. During this time, he came to recognize the plight of the big game population on Newfoundland's Great Northern Peninsula. After nine years as a forest warden, he became a wildlife protection officer with the Newfoundland Wildlife Service.

For seventeen years, he has devoted his efforts to the growth and conservation of the big game population on the Great Northern Peninsula. Under his surveillance, the moose and caribou populations have grown and prospered at an astonishing rate. As a game warden and a local storyteller, he has gained the respect of conservationist and poacher alike.

He has been presented with a number of awards: the Safari International, presented by the Provincial Wildlife Division; the Gunther Behr, presented by the Newfoundland and Labrador Wildlife Federation; and the Achievement "Beyond the Call of Duty" Award, presented by the White Bay Central Development Association.

His previous books, *Will Anyone Search for Danny?* and *The Price Paid for Charley,* have become Canadian bestsellers.

He is married to the former Beatrice Compton of Englee. They have four children, and make their home in Roddickton, Newfoundland.

PROLOGUE

Blood on the Hills

(1)　We can almost hear a cry that's unheard by the
　　　　drums of mortal man.
　　　It's the sound of the unborn caribou as they
　　　　move o'er the frozen land.
　　　They tumble & roll in their liquid home and kick
　　　　for lack of space,
　　　But they're unaware of their terrible fate when
　　　　they meet the human race.

(2)　"I'm cramped and confined in this watery sack;
　　　　my hoofs are around my ears,
　　　"And I've been in this place for a long, long time;
　　　　it seems to be like years.
　　　"I have to get out for it's time to go and get my
　　　　feet on the ground."
　　　But it's all controlled by his mother with her
　　　　movement, sight and sound.

(3)　It's late in May and it's 7:00 a.m. as the unborn
　　　　turns in its cell.
　　　It can feel the warmth from the morning sun as
　　　　its mom feeds on the hill.
　　　It can hear the noise of the great outdoors and
　　　　wonders what made that sound.
　　　Then a blasting roar from a rifle, and his mother
　　　　falls to the ground.

(4)   "Mom – oh mom – what has happened? Can you
        hear me this mother of mine?
"Oh mother, am I about to be born; will this
        morning be my time?"
Then he heard the sound of an engine and a
        voice called out, "Hey Joe.
"Good shootin' my son, good shootin'. This one is
        a big old doe."

(5)   "Hurry up! Paunch her, Calvin! John Christian
        may come around."
And in less than a minute the unborn calf was
        dumped out on the ground.
It tries to stand with shivering legs and looks at
        the men as they kill,
Then it drops in a heap by its mother and is now
        part of *Blood on the Hills*.

Earl B. Pilgrim

Table of Contents

Prologue

1. The Arrest of Calvin Pollard 1

2. The Grey Islands Decoy 16

3. A Gift from Sears 21

4. Ryland Gill's Secret Cache 33

5. Stakeout Near Cat Cove 37

6. Blood on the Hills 44

7. The Soufflets River Chase 52

8. The Cat Cove Stakeout Continued 68

9. Rendezvous at Cat Cove 79

10. The Hydro Plant 84

11. The Port au Choix Incident 91

12. The Twin Calves 102

13. The Wildlife Racket 107

14. Luke Greene Confesses 122

15. Ryland Gill 133

Epilogue 137

Chapter 1

The Arrest of Calvin Pollard

Thursday, February 7, 1985, dawned a beautiful day. It was cold and crisp. Looking out the window just after dawn, Wildlife Officer John Christian could tell from the streaks of light shining through the trees that the sun would momentarily send its brilliant rays over Roddickton, a northern Newfoundland town based on the forest resources of the hinterland. Chimney smoke was rising straight up into the frosty air, indicating that there wasn't even a breath of wind. Christian put the kettle on the stove and started to prepare breakfast. At such an early hour, few people were moving around the White Bay town. Those on the move were mainly loggers on their way to work in the bush.

He was just sitting down to eat breakfast when the telephone rang.

Lifting the receiver, he said, "Hello."

"Hey, John, is that you?" asked the voice on the other end of the line.

"Yes, it is."

1

"It's Ed Walsh here," the caller said. Ed Walsh, the corporal in charge of the Migratory Bird Section on Newfoundland's west coast, worked hand-in-hand with the provincial wildlife officers.

"Good morning, Ed," John greeted him.

"Good morning. What's the weather like up your way?"

"It's just a glorious morning up here. It's cold and clear, with not a breath of wind. Where are you, anyway?"

John was excited now. Usually after a call from Ed Walsh, he became involved in some way or other in a memorable incident on a patrol. They had worked together on many cases, and had just closed a file that ended in their catching a group of men with a moose they had killed illegally; they laid ten charges.

"I'm in Corner Brook," Walsh replied.

Newfoundland's second largest city, Corner Brook is located along eleven kilometres of shoreline on the southern side of Humber Arm, Bay of Islands.

"Listen, John," Ed continued. "I was trying to get in touch with you last night, but there was no answer. Our helicopter is coming up there this morning, and will be taking Terry Legg to Cat Cove."

Corporal Legg was the N.C.O. in charge of the detachment of the Royal Canadian Mounted Police at Roddickton, which was staffed by three members.

"He has to go up there to serve a subpoena," Ed continued. "I told him to make sure to get in touch with you, so the two of you can do a combined patrol. Terry said he'd be only too glad to do that."

"Now, that's a great idea!" John said. "It's a perfect morning for a helicopter patrol. I'd say there are quite a few people in the country today."

"Maybe so," Walsh replied.

"What time is the helicopter leaving Corner Brook?" John asked.

"In just a few minutes."

"Okay, Ed. I'll get in touch with Terry right away. Thanks a million!"

"No problem, John, boy! Glad to be of service."

"Goodbye."

Right away, Christian called the Roddickton Detachment of the R.C.M.P. and talked with Corporal Legg, who confirmed that the helicopter was on its way to the town. He was glad to hear from the wildlife officer, and agreed they should do a combined patrol of the area.

"When the machine arrives," he promised, "I'll give you a shout. Don't go anywhere!"

"Okay," John said. "I'll stay here and wait. Goodbye."

Before long, he heard the sound of an approaching helicopter. By eight o'clock, it had landed on the police station grounds.

He received a call from Corporal Legg, telling him to come over. "We'll be leaving shortly," he said.

Gathering together the things he would need—his folding pad containing statement forms, caution sheets, a writing pad, camera, and winter clothes, including snowshoes—John proceeded to the station.

He soon saw the blue-and-white Long Ranger helicopter, parked near the detachment building. Inside the station, he met Corporal Legg and the helicopter pilot, Corporal Woods, who was from British Columbia. He was also introduced to Joe Green, a young constable who hailed from Sheet Harbour, Nova Scotia, and had recently been posted to Roddickton.

Tall, well-built and fine-looking, he appeared to be disciplined and capable of looking after himself.

"John," Corporal Legg said, "I'm sorry, but I'm unable to go with you today. There's been a slight change of plans. We had a report of flares being sighted last night off Englee. There may be someone in distress."

Situated on the east side of the Great Northern Peninsula, Englee lies in a sheltered harbour on the northern headland of Canada Bay.

"The call came in just a few minutes ago," the corporal explained, "so Joe will be going with you instead of myself. Here's what you can do..."

The R.C.M.P. and the provincial wildlife officers in Newfoundland had an excellent working relationship. This day would turn out to be another prime example.

Huddled together, they were briefed by Corporal Legg about the plan. Their first instruction was to check White Bay for the source of the flares. Then they were to go out near the Grey Islands—two large islands, Bell Island and Groais Island—located in White Bay, east of Englee. After that, they were to move on to the Cat Cove area to serve the subpoena for Corporal Legg. While they were out patrolling, he would travel to Englee and obtain an account from the people who had reported the flares.

Checking their notebooks and other equipment, they went outside to the waiting helicopter. Constable Green decided to sit in the front, and John sat in the rear. Each of them put on a set of headphones, ensuring clear communication with each other. Once they fastened their seat belts, they were ready to leave. They lifted off at nine o'clock.

They headed out toward the ocean via Englee, a town with a population of approximately thirteen hundred people. The whole town seemed to be on the move, taking advantage of the promising sunny day. Every year at this time, men cutting their next winter's firewood could be seen wherever there was a sizeable stand of trees. This day was no exception. They also saw numerous children on their way to school, and women pinning laundry on their clotheslines. The armada of boats at the marine centre looked like goodies stacked on the shelves in a Christmas toy store.

Flying over Barr'd Island, they were at the edge of the Atlantic Ocean. They could see very little open water anywhere; the ocean was almost completely frozen over.

They moved on, flying low. Their conversation was limited to sparse comments about the ice, and what they were really looking for—someone in distress.

They flew near the Grey Islands and, later, the Horse Islands, but saw nothing out of the ordinary, although they spent considerable time in the area. Pilot Woods decided to halt the search and continue on to Cat Cove.

Reaching land, they flew inland for fifteen or so miles, and from there turned southwest for a straight-line search toward Cat Cove. Having much experience in that area, John pinpointed the spot where he thought they should conduct a check.

He commented that most poaching took place in bad weather, either early in the morning or shortly before dark. For this reason, he explained that he didn't think they would catch anyone poaching on this day. "The weather is too good," he said. "Our chances of catching a poacher at ten o'clock on a clear, wind-free morning are extremely slim."

"Hey, Woods!" he said suddenly. "Take a look at that area to your left. If any tracks are seen there, they're guaranteed to belong to someone who's hunting." The partridge hunting season had opened only two days before.

"Okay," Woods said, "but I don't have very much time. We've got to serve the subpoena, then get right back to Roddickton. We'll have a quick look around here before moving on."

"Good!" Christian said excitedly. "That'll be okay with me." They kept their eyes glued to the ground for signs of snowmobile tracks. The pilot turned the helicopter in the direction he had indicated.

They had travelled only a couple of miles when John spotted, in the distance, the tracks of a snowmobile.

"Hey, boys!" he shouted above the sound of the helicopter. "Look up ahead! There are some snow-mobile tracks!"

"What? Where?" Green and Woods asked in unison.

"Right straight ahead!"

"Okay, okay," they said. "We can see them now."

They quickly moved in over the area where the telltale tracks were located.

"Listen, guys," John said as they got nearer, "these tracks are fresh."

"They seem that way," Pilot Woods said.

"Hey, look!" John shouted as he pointed with his finger. "Their tracks are coming in on that brook. To your left! To your left!"

Woods expertly banked his craft to the left; the blades made a chopping sound.

"Hey, Joe!" Christian called to Constable Green. "Look! Two Ski-doos right there on the brook to your left, and they're almost directly underneath us!"

He peered below. "Yes," he said, "I see them..."

Suddenly, Woods interrupted. "A moose! Right under us in the woods! Look! It's killed! See the steam rising out of it?"

"Where?" John asked, disbelievingly. Then he saw it. "Stop the helicopter! Put her down!"

"Just a second," the pilot said as he manoeuvred the controls, "until I get her around again." As Woods spoke, the Long Ranger swung around smoothly. "Look!" he said. "Do you still see it?"

"Yes," John answered. "Now, guys, we've got to catch these poachers. I've had plenty of experience at this, so I'll tell you what to do. We have to find a way to corner them on the brook."

"Okay," Woods said. "What do we do now?"

This was Green's first patrol in the Roddickton area, his first ever wildlife patrol, and he was intrigued by this entirely new process.

From his back seat on the chopper, John surveyed the area, his mind working feverishly. Noticing a valley about half a mile downriver, he realized this would be the poachers' only means of escape. But he knew he would still have to bluff them in some way.

"Now, Woods," he said, "can you land on that open space on the other side, by the brook?"

"Sure." Woods found the spot and landed.

"Everybody stay aboard," John said. "The poachers will probably think we're putting someone out. We've done this before, and it has worked."

They waited a minute or two. "Now," he told the pilot. "Take her up."

They lifted off.

"Now, Woods," he said, "put me down on the brook."

They travelled down the brook approximately half a mile to a small frozen steady, the only place in the entire area where a helicopter could land.

Once the pilot had set the chopper down, John instructed his co-workers about their next step.

"Go back, find the men, and keep the machine hovering right over them until I get there."

"Okay," they said, "we'll do that."

He climbed out, put on his snowshoes and began walking up the brook.

After walking about a hundred yards, he noticed moose hair and a spot of blood on the trail. The tracks indicated that a second moose had been killed on the trail and removed to another site.

He moved swiftly up the brook in the tracks of the two snowmobiles, carefully peering around every bend in the trail and making mental plans. He decided that if the snowmobiles came toward him, he would tackle one of the men, take his machine and use it to run down and catch the second fellow. He heard the helicopter, as he noticed that the blood from the second moose led up into the valley in which he had to corner and trap the men. He was sure he had an excellent chance of catching them.

The helicopter roared overhead. Green and Woods kept their eyes on John creeping up the brook. Soon, he would be close enough to see the poachers.

Green pointed to a large tree nearby. On the ground, Christian saw two snowmobiles on the brook and snapped a picture of them.

He walked into the woods toward the two poachers. They were hiding under a tree, their backs turned to him. He reached for his camera and took another shot. The men were unaware that anyone was approaching them from the ground; their only concern was remaining hidden from the helicopter's occupants.

John walked over to one of the men and tapped him on the shoulder. Startled, he whirled around. A look of disbelief registered on his face. He certainly hadn't expected to see the officer! John knew him, but was unable to call him by name.

The other man, realizing something was wrong, swung around. John recognized him immediately. He was Joseph "Joe" Gill, who had been convicted in court shortly before, on a charge John had laid against him.

"John," he said resignedly. "We're caught."

"Yes, I guess you are," the officer said.

John walked out of the woods, onto the brook, and waved for Green and Woods to continue down to the place where they had put him off.

He returned to the two men. Looking at the one he knew, John said, "Mr. Gill, I'm going to caution you." He read him his rights and informed him he was under arrest.

He then asked the other man to tell him his name. "Calvin Pollard."

He cautioned Pollard, read him his rights and placed him under arrest.

Next, he seized their snowmobiles. The men accompanied the officer to one of the moose—a large cow—that had been killed. They admitted to killing the animal.

"John," Joe Gill said, "I'm glad you caught me this way, and not like before when you caught me in my home. You know that was a cowardly thing to do, don't you?"

"Well," John countered, "why didn't you learn your lesson then? Look at the mess you're in now!"

He complained about the Wildlife Service and what he called "the laws of the land," but Christian paid no attention to him.

He found a twelve-gauge shotgun, the weapon Gill and Pollard admitted to having used to kill the animal.

"Okay," he said, "here's what you two are going to do. Both of you are going out on one snowmobile, following me. You're not to go on ahead or leave me. I'm reminding you—you're both under arrest, and you must do as I say."

The trio went down the brook to where the helicopter had landed. Pilot Woods informed John that he was unable to assist him any further. This forced him to make alternate plans. He briefed Constable Green so that they could plan their next move.

They decided that poacher Joe Gill would go on with Green and Woods to Cat Cove, where Green would obtain a statement from him.

He asked Green to call Clarence Maloney, his supervisor at Pasadena, and have him come to Cat Cove in a helicopter to assist in the case. Green was happy to comply, taking some of the work off John's shoulders.

Green and Woods left with Gill, leaving John with Pollard and the two snowmobiles.

When the helicopter disappeared from sight, he asked Pollard to tell him who had shot the second moose. He said he didn't know.

They left on the snowmobiles, following the blood and tracks up the brook. Officer Christian turned to the right and spotted, approximately three hundred yards ahead, the paunch of the other slain animal. It was a bull, and the only parts left were its head, legs and paunch. From the size of the head and teeth, he figured it must have been ten years old.

John and Pollard went back to the first kill. Stopping their snowmobiles, they walked to the spot where the cow had been killed.

He knew Calvin Pollard wasn't a big-time poacher. In fact, he was surprised to even see him in the country.

"Calvin," John said, "do you really know what you've done?"

He looked at the officer. John could tell by the expression on Pollard's face that he was feeling ashamed.

"What do you mean?" he asked innocently.

"Calvin, you've killed a large cow. Do you know why she didn't run?"

"No, I don't know."

"Well, I'm going to *show* you the reason she was unable to run." He asked Pollard to pass him the knife.

John took out the paunch and rolled it over, revealing the sac that contained a fetus. The cow moose had been between four and five months pregnant. Pollard watched him closely.

He slit a hole in the sac. Putting his hand inside, he felt around for the head of the unborn animal. The steam was still visible in the frosty morning air. He pulled the head from the sac and looked at Pollard. Pollard could hardly believe his eyes.

"Look at this, Calvin," John ordered. "Can you see what you've destroyed? This is why that poor cow couldn't run!"

He carefully pulled the animal all the way out of its mother's body and held it up. It was still attached by the cord to the sac.

11

"This is what you've done, Calvin," he said. "Look at it!"

"John," he gasped, "I never realized! Boy, oh boy! It's awful!"

Severing the cord, he placed the unborn calf on its mother's head and snapped several pictures.

Pollard was in a sorry state by now. John knew he was ready to tell him who had killed the other moose.

"Calvin," he said, "will you give me a cautioned statement?"

"Yes."

He cautioned Pollard and read him his rights. He told the officer that he and his buddy, Joe Gill, had seen and shot the moose while they were hunting partridges.

He asked if Pollard had had a licence the previous fall.

He said he did, and he had killed a large bull.

"Then, why are you in hunting now?" he asked, a touch of irritation in his voice.

Pollard admitted he didn't have an answer to the questions.

John asked him more questions about the killings, and he now revealed the details of the whole story.

Both of them—officer and poacher—cleaned the moose and dragged it by hand out to the brook. They cut the animal in four pieces, attached the quarters to one of the snowmobiles and hauled them down to the steady. They packed the meat well, making it ready to be picked up later by the helicopter.

Finished, they moved down Kellys Brook toward the salt water.

Half a mile later, they saw the tracks of two more moose hunters. Immediately, John started after them.

The hunters ran out over the frozen brook, dropping their guns behind them. Having a head start, they soon disappeared from sight.

John slowed down to secure the safety of his prisoner. Continuing, they tracked the blood on the trail across Northwest Arm for at least three miles to an area where firewood was being cut. John spotted where the men had buried the moose before removing it and hauling it toward town.

He looked at his watch. It was almost 3:00 p.m. Realizing he couldn't follow up this new development, he had no choice but to abandon the chase and concentrate on the case at hand.

He and Pollard arrived in Cat Cove half an hour later. He was not sure if Green had relayed the message to his supervisor. Nor did he know what kind of situation he would be walking into at Cat Cove.

He was met by a number of men as he walked through town. Cat Cove residents are fine people. The men act like real men, and not like boys. They didn't accept the maxim "If you touch one, you touch all." If individuals got caught poaching—or doing anything else they shouldn't be doing—they were on their own to face their punishment.

They stopped on the ice in front of the government wharf. "John," Pollard said, "come on up to my house for a lunch. You must be starving by now."

"Yes, I am." All he could do was to look at Pollard in amazement!

What kind of man is this at all? he wondered.

It was then that they heard a helicopter coming; it was for him and it was drawing near.

"No, Calvin," John said. "Thanks all the same. You're free to go now. You're no longer under arrest."

He looked at the officer. "Can I have my axe and snowshoes?" he asked. "They're all I have to get firewood."

"Yes," John said, "I don't see any reason why you can't have them back. Take them."

Pollard took them and left.

Clarence Maloney, John's supervisor, arrived on the scene. He stepped out of the Jet Ranger helicopter, and asked what they should do about the situation.

Christian told him they would have to move fairly fast, as they had only an hour and a half before nightfall. "We'll have to take the two snowmobiles and move them back to a hill about five to ten miles out," he said. "Then we'll have to map out the spot and put the moose in the same place. Tomorrow we'll fly the machines and moose across to Hawke's Bay, approximately fifty miles across the peninsula."

A lumbering community, Hawke's Bay is located on the southeastern side of a bay by the identical name, an inlet of Ingornachoix Bay, on the Great Northern Peninsula.

Maloney agreed to the plan.

They put the snowmobiles in a sling, and the helicopter took them away. In fifteen minutes, it returned for John; he and the pilot picked up the moose on Kellys Brook to stash them with the snowmobiles.

Going back to Cat Cove, they picked up Clarence Maloney, then headed for Hawke's Bay via the cut right-of-way along Cat Cove Brook. They talked about the poaching problems they were experiencing as a result of the partridge hunting season being open at this time of the year. Suddenly, something below them caught John's eyes.

"Hey, Clarence!" he said. "Look there! A kill! Look at the blood!" He pointed to the area he was talking about.

"You're right, ol' man!" Clarence said. "You're right!" Calling to the pilot, he said. "Hey, put down the chopper for a moment."

"Okay," said the pilot, "but we can only stay for a minute or two. It's getting dark."

"No problem."

John jumped out as the helicopter landed. Right away he spotted what the moose had been killed with—buckshot. There were shot pellets strewn on the snow. He picked up five empty shot shells. Looking closer, he found a cut-off shell. Hunters used these to kill moose because the cut shell travelled like a ball. The shot, trapped in the plastic case, acted like a slug and became a deadly weapon.

He noted that the moose was a large bull, and that the meat had been taken to Cat Cove. He spied a pair of white nylon gloves near the kill; these had been used to paunch the animal, after which they were left with the paunch. "Oh, oh," he thought. "Whoever did this would have a set of clean hands, if checked."

Disgusted, he jumped into the helicopter. He dropped the spent shells into his pocket and put on the headphones. As they lifted off, he complained again to Clarence about the partridge hunting season. He agreed with John that it should never have been opened.

On Thursday, April 4, 1985, Joe Gill and Calvin Pollard appeared in court. They pleaded guilty as charged. Their statements were read, and they were convicted.

The presiding judge gave Calvin a $1,000.00 fine, declaring that he was prohibited from holding a big game licence for five years and that his snowmobile was to be forfeited to the Crown.

Chapter 2

The Grey Islands Decoy:
A Great Plan Except for the Weather

Wildlife had served a notice of intent on Joseph Gill before the court date. Before sentencing, the officers explained how they had caught Gill once before.

A year previously, the officers were working frantically to protect the wildlife in the Cat Cove area. Conducting a survey, they found only a few moose there. They realized that if they were to have a moose population in the Roddickton–St. Anthony area, they would have to obtain their breeding stock from the Cat Cove resource, as small as it was.

Some years earlier, the Department of Forestry had introduced moose by truck to the Roddickton area. At that time, John Christian worked as a Forest Ranger. One moose—a cow with calf—died less than half a mile from where it was released. The other, a bull, had succeeded in travelling approximately twenty miles north, where it was run down and shot near Bear Cove.

The wildlife officers knew they would encounter stiff opposition. They struck hard at poachers, creating many enemies in the process. Even some of John's closest friends told him he was going too far.

He became friends with Dr. Gorden W. Thomas, then executive director of the International Grenfell Association. He encouraged John, backing him with his Association's resources.

Judge Robert Jenkins, now retired, understood their job, and knew what a wildlife population meant to the province of Newfoundland and Labrador. In this regard, he had given many poachers their just desserts. Poachers actually had a nickname for him—Wildlife Jenkins! When storms were howling and the lamplight was flickering at night, Judge Jenkins was the prime topic of conversation in many poachers' cabins, especially if someone under the roof was scheduled for a court appearance.

Unfortunately, even with a strict court, air surveillance, and ground patrols, the residents of Cat Cove were still beating them to the punch. John chatted with the prominent people in the town, but the poaching didn't stop. For years, their supervisor, Norman Muise, was as puzzled as his officers were at their lack of success.

An informant told the local officers that somebody in Roddickton was watching them closely and giving the Cat Cove poachers the information they needed. They talked the situation over, then met with Muise. They decided they should be as smart as the poachers were. "If we can't outwit them," they reasoned, "then we have no right to call ourselves wildlife officers."

In Roddickton, there was a leak in the telephone systems. Some people had radios with certain bands.

They would tune in the microwave tower, then place the radio receiver, with its back facing west, on the floor near an electrical outlet. When the radio was turned on, they would listen to conversations. As one party finished their conversation and replaced the receiver, another would cut in. With four or five of these radios in operation, most conversations could be monitored easily.

Wildlife Officer John Christian reported one such party to the R.C.M.P., who then investigated and confirmed that this was happening. Consequently, the phone company installed a scrambler on their equipment, so he was told.

They decided to use the informants against the poachers. Since the snitches were reporting Wildlife's movements to the poachers for their illegal activities, it was only poetic justice for Wildlife to use *them* in spreading false information back to their masters!

They set out to fool the suspects and their informants by planning a fake duck-hunting trip to the Grey Islands, eighteen miles offshore from Englee. The officers planned to give everyone the impression they were going to be far away on their own weekend of rest and relaxation. They hoped to lure the poachers into a false sense of security. Then, they planned to circle the killing grounds and apprehend the poachers from inland.

The officers gave their week-long trip extensive publicity. John got in touch with the person who was giving the Cat Cove poachers information regarding their whereabouts. He made sure he knew the date and time he and his friends were leaving for their weekend trip.

They created a great deal of confusion by borrowing guns and driving around town with their duck decoys in full view. Eric Kinden, the Forestry Technician, and now a fisheries officer who had sacrificed greatly by working nights and weekends, taking much verbal abuse in the process, took his annual leave to be part of their operation. They laid their plans carefully.

On Friday afternoon, Kinden and John would go to the Grey Islands with Rex Boyd, using a Cessna 185 from Belvey Aviation. Around nine o' clock on Saturday morning, Norman Muise and another wildlife officer would go by helicopter to the Cat Cove area. If they struck on anything positive, they would send Rex Boyd to the Grey Islands and bring Kinden and Christian back. But they were to remain there until something unusual happened.

The only way to reach the Grey Islands in the winter is by airplane. They went to the Grey Islands and settled in their cabin. It snowed on Saturday, a little mild, but still cool. They sat around the cabin, listening to the radio, and checking the time periodically. The weather was perfect for poachers. "What a day the boys will have poaching!" one of them said.

At Cormack, Norman Muise awoke early. Looking through the window, he noticed the snow. *This is a good morning,* he thought, *for the boys at Cat Cove. They're guaranteed to be in at the moose today.*

Still in his underwear, Norman picked up the phone receiver and called the helicopter pilot, John Ennis.

"Hey, John," he said when he got a response. "It's a pretty good morning for poaching, isn't it?"

"I haven't looked out yet," Ennis said sleepily. "Have you?"

"Yes," Norman said. "It's snowing here." He lived at Cormack, eighteen kilometres north of Deer Lake at the base of the Great Northern Peninsula. It was about twenty miles from Pasadena, where the pilot lived.

"How bad is it?" Ennis asked.

"Oh, not too bad," Norman replied. "I don't think it's anything to stop us from flying."

"Have you heard the forecast this morning?"

"No, but it looks mild. There are big blossoms of snow falling."

Ennis had concerns. "I hope it doesn't get bad enough to freeze on the blade."

"My son, are you losing your nerve?" Norman asked loudly, in a joking tone of voice.

Ennis laughed. "I'm getting up now," he said. "There isn't much need of us going in too early. You could scare these guys off."

"I know," Norman said. "How about if we left here around eight? I figure we should be up there just in time to grab any poachers."

"Okay, I'll pick you up at eight."

"Great! Great!" Norman said, hanging up the receiver.

While Muise and Ennis were up and getting mobile, Eric Kinden and John Christian were forced to hang around the Grey Islands all Saturday. After the snow in the morning, they had freezing rain. They knew this was excellent poaching weather. Christian hoped this wasn't the case around Cat Cove, and areas south. Freezing rain was the deadliest enemy to winter flying. Pilots were always on alert for this kind of condition, and refused to take any chances at these times. He also knew that if the weather got too bad, it would prevent Norman Muise from reaching the area. They relaxed, put on a big feed of salt beef and potatoes, all the while listening to *Basic Black* on the Canadian Broadcasting Corporation.

20

Chapter 3

A Gift from Sears

The helicopter picked up Norman Muise at 8:00 a.m. near his Cormack home. The slam-bang of the rotors caused his neighbours to dash to their windows. They wondered aloud to each other, "Norm must be at something very important to be on the move with a helicopter on this stormy morning. I wonder where he's headed."

Norman Muise's neighbourhood wasn't the dullest or loneliest place in the world. He and his wife had ten children, and each one of them was rough, ready and able. Mrs. Muise, a distinguished lady, always found time amid her busy schedule to prepare a fine meal for everyone who walked into her kitchen. Norman, one of the most highly respected game wardens in the country, had done tremendous work in helping to build up and maintain the big game populations of Newfoundland. He exhibited fearless will and great determination.

"What do you think of it, John?" Norman asked as he hopped aboard the aircraft.

"'Tis pretty thick," Ennis answered slowly, checking the instruments on the panel before him.

"I'd say the best way to go is to follow the highway to Jackson's Arm, then follow the shoreline."

"I'd say that's the right way, too. At least we'll know where we're headed. 'Twill be better than going inside, overland."

"You're right."

The pilot coaxed his helicopter forward at a cautious speed. The men were alert. The cliffs along the east coast of the Great Northern Peninsula were perpendicular, almost a thousand feet high, with fjords similar to those found on the coast of Norway. A pilot flying in this area had to be alert at all times for downdrafts from high off the towering mountains. This was why John Ennis was picked so often to fly wildlife patrols. He had the necessary experience.

"Norm," he said as he dodged the cliffs, "the rain's starting to freeze on. Just look at the rotors."

Norman looked out. "You're right," he said gravely.

Ennis wheeled the craft around. At the same time, he said, "It seems to be getting a bit worse."

The helicopter moved along, hugging the shoreline as it headed back toward Jackson's Arm. Now they noticed the ice beginning to fall from the rotors.

"Maybe we should go in over the hills."

"Okay," Ennis agreed. "We'll try it."

The helicopter climbed the side of the mountain, then flew inland, following the valleys. It continued northwest for twelve miles.

"The rain is freezing on again, Norm, boy," Ennis said.

"Maybe we should put her down on one of the ponds and wait awhile," Norman suggested.

"I don't know that we should. This stuff could be on for days."

"Okay, John. I'll tell you what we should do. Let's go back and do a patrol in the Hampden area. Maybe the conditions up here might improve." Hampden is a lumbering community at the head of White Bay.

"That's fine," Ennis said as he turned the helicopter.

As the machine moved slowly south, the ice was dropping from its body. The craft seemed to be screaming at the valleys below.

Norman Muise didn't get to Cat Cove that day. The weather conditions prevented the helicopter from performing its work, but it was perfect for the poachers, who were very busy all day long.

Muise and Ennis rescheduled their plans to the following morning. They left early; the day was clear, but still cool. The snow had stopped falling just after dark the night before. The helicopter flew low over open country up the peninsula, the occupants looking for the signs of snowmobiles.

"Go over to that area," Norman said, pointing with his hand.

"Okay," Ennis said.

They moved cautiously.

"Look!" Norman suddenly said. "Did you see that crow?"

"Where?"

"Keep her over! Keep her over!" Norman commanded as he continued to point.

Ennis quickly turned the helicopter in the direction Norman was indicating. "Yes!" he shouted. "I see it now."

They flew on in silence for a few more minutes.

23

"There's something killed here for sure," Norman said.

"Look over there," Ennis said, "a whole slew of crows!"

"You're right, John. Look at the snowmobile tracks. They're on the tracks of moose."

"Hold it, Norm! Look at the blood!"

"Look at the paunch!"

"Yes, I see it. And there's another paunch over there."

Ennis slowly circled the craft around the area. He and Norman counted four paunches in that one area alone. They checked the four kills, and all of them were moose.

"Yesterday," Norman said.

"Sure was," Ennis agreed.

"If only we had gotten up here. John Christian was right. They're gone out to Cat Cove, too."

"Looks like all of the meat's removed."

"Just take a look around."

"Okay."

They circled the area where the kills had taken place.

"Hey, John!" Norman said in surprise. "Look there!" He pointed to a stand of timber. "Put her down in that open area right there. I want to have a closer look."

"Okay."

The pilot landed his helicopter in the snow. Norman jumped out. He put on his snowshoes and disappeared into the woods in the area where the men had had lunch, after killing the moose. He surveyed the area, but the men had left no clues that he could see. He kicked the cold fireplace. "If only we could have gotten here yesterday," he muttered.

He turned to walk away. Suddenly, he spotted a piece of paper on the snow near a tree. He stooped down and picked it up. It was crumpled into a ball. He tried to unfold the wad, but it was frozen together.

Frustrated, he walked back to the helicopter.

"The men from Cat Cove have done it again," he told Ennis, "and they got away with it too. Christian was right. If only the weather had been in our favour yesterday."

"Did you get any clue at all?" the pilot asked. "Have you got any ideas?"

"Not one thing," Norman said disgustedly.

"What should we do?"

Norman sat still for five minutes, thinking, *Should we go on to Cat Cove? Follow these tracks in?*

"No," he said aloud, answering his own thoughts.

He remembered the piece of paper in his hand and started to unfold it. The warm air in the helicopter made the task a little easier.

"Just a minute," he said, "let's take a look at this."

All of his concentration was focused on the scrap of paper. The engine was roaring. The wind from the rotors was whipping up the snow, yet nothing but the paper seemed to attract Norman's attention.

"Oh yes, Johnny, my boy!" he shouted. "We might have something here after all!" As he spoke, he slowly unrolled the paper.

"Yes!" he said. "Look at this! Sears! This piece of paper came off a parcel that came in the mail!"

"It sure did," John shouted over the headset.

"Well, look here," Norman continued. "A person's name!" He unrolled the paper a little more.

"Look, Norm, there are pieces of bread falling out of the paper."

25

"Yes," Norman replied. "The men had their sandwiches or bread wrapped up in this."

"You're right!"

"Here's the name," Norman said. "Mrs. Mary Pollard, Cat Cove, Newfoundland!"

They stared at the name.

Norman was the first to speak. "This might be our clue," he said. "Someone had their lunch wrapped up in this, then threw the paper away. Christian's the right one to work on this!"

"I'd say you're right," Ennis said.

"We won't go any closer to town right now," Norman said. "We might disturb someone. They're guaranteed to have their refrigerators full. Nobody knows how many moose they've killed. They've got four of them here alone!"

"What are they going to do with all that meat?" Ennis asked. "I mean—with all that they're bringing out of the woods."

"They've got to be selling it," Norman said. "There's no way they can be eating it."

"Maybe you're right."

"Okay, let's head back toward the Hampden area."

"Good enough."

The pilot headed the helicopter back, the engine roaring in the cool morning air. The men knew two things for certain. Nobody had seen them, and they had an important clue—someone's name inscribed on a piece of paper from Sears.

Norman looked at the name again, then jotted it down in his notebook. "You never know," he said. "This might be the key."

Pilot Ennis said nothing, his attention focused on the horizon and the barrens zipping past below.

On Grey Island, John Christian remained in the cabin all day Sunday, cooking the meals. Eric Kinden had killed six eider, shore ducks, on Saturday. They had two for lunch on Sunday. They were still waiting for something to happen, but nothing did until midafternoon when Rex Boyd arrived. They quickly gathered their gear together and went outside to meet him.

"John," Rex said, "your wife called and told me you are to come right away. She said no more. And Norm Muise called."

"I guess Norm must have spotted something."

"John, what a day yesterday was for poaching!" Rex said. "I'd say they got everything killed around Cat Cove this weekend!"

"I hope some of them got caught," Christian replied. "Have you heard anything?"

"No. If they did get caught, I would have heard something. Don't worry, they would have been screaming by now."

"Maybe they didn't catch anyone. Anyway, we'll see."

They boarded the Cessna 185 and flew to Main Brook. From Main Brook, Rex drove them by car to Roddickton.

John arrived home late. His wife wasn't at home, but there was a message waiting for him to call Norman Muise immediately. Knowing there was something in the air, he went to the phone.

"John," Norman said, "they made an awful slaughter! They came up Bloody Alley." Christian and Norman had given it this name a few years earlier because of the trail of hair and blood from the poached moose and caribou that led the entire way to Cat Cove.

"Did you catch anyone?" John asked angrily.

"No," he said bluntly.

"Have you got any clues?"

Norman stopped for a moment. "Yes, I have one clue, John."

"What is it?"

"One of the fellows had his lunch wrapped in a piece of paper. There's a name on the paper. The paper came off a Sears parcel. You know, the kind that comes in the mail." He paused. "Just a second, John," he continued. "I'll get my notebook."

"Okay."

"Now, let's see," Norman said when he returned to the phone. "Oh, here it is. A Mrs. Mary Pollard."

"Well, well," John said. "It's a clue all right!" He stopped and scratched his head. "I don't know anyone by that name," he said. "Maybe she's one of the older people."

"Maybe so," Norman said, "but get to work on it, will you?"

"I sure will."

He got the telephone directory, found Cat Cove under the Jackson's Arm Exchange, and read through the names. There were many Pollards listed.

He called the Roddickton R.C.M.P., telling them what they had found and asking them to check at a certain place.

"I certainly will," the corporal on duty said, "and I'll get right back to you."

"Great," he said.

Fifteen minutes later, the phone rang. John grabbed the receiver.

"R.C.M.P. here," the corporal said.

"Oh, yes," he said. "Find anything?"

"Yes, I did. Mary Pollard is sixty-three years old, and her husband Henry is sixty-six."

"I wonder if he has any sons?" John said.

"I don't know."

"Okay. I'll have to phone our source at Cat Cove."

"It's all right if you can trust him."

"No problem there. The only thing is, can he get the information we need without alerting anyone?"

John agreed that there was a risk. "You've got a good point there, but I have no choice. We've got to gamble now, anyway."

"I guess so."

"I'll let you know what happens."

"Good," the R.C.M.P. officer said as he replaced the receiver.

John sat for awhile, again scratching his head. "Yes," he said aloud, "this is our only key to finding out the connection, or who was involved with Henry Pollard." He was puzzled, because he knew Henry Pollard wasn't a name associated with poaching.

"Here goes," he said as he picked up the receiver and started dialing a familiar number. The phone rang twice.

"Hello," a man answered.

"John Christian here," he said.

"I was expecting you to call. There's a bloody trail west of here, and the men were on the move all Saturday night."

"Got any names for me?"

"Not for sure."

"I've got a clue," the officer told him. He gave him the name from the Sears wrapper, filling him in on what had happened.

He laughed. "John," he said, "I'll get back to you."

29

"Okay."

John had a quick shower and was starting to write a few notes when the phone rang. He picked it up.

"Hello," the voice on the other end said, "'tis me again. John, my son! You're on the right track all right, and if you make the right moves, you can catch the whole works—and more besides!"

"Well, what did you find out?"

"I did some checking. Mary Pollard had a parcel come in the mail last week. I found out something else, too, and this might be the one thing you're looking for."

"What is it?" John asked anxiously. He sat down, his pen and notebook ready.

"Well," his informant said, "on Friday night, Mary Pollard's youngest daughter had her boyfriend over to her house. Around eleven-thirty, the young man got ready to go home. As he was leaving the house, he asked Mrs. Pollard if she had an extra loaf of bread to spare because he and a bunch of his buddies were going in the country, and his mother didn't have any baked bread. Mrs. Pollard gave him a loaf. She wrapped it up in a piece of paper that came off a C.O.D. parcel she had received a couple of days before from Sears. Then the young man left the house and went on home. And, John, guess what?"

"What, boy?"

"That's the piece of paper you got!"

This stroke of luck was so bizarre it was funny. He could only laugh. "Give me some names," he said.

"It was young Walter Ropson," he said.

Christian scribbled down the name.

"John," he said, "I know who went hunting with him Saturday morning. It was Jack Gill. That's Joe's son. The other three lads were from up in the other bottom—Jerry Greene, Stan Simms, and you know who—the fellow who's involved with the whole thing, Ryland Gill."

"That's what I figured. They're sending their sons in to poach for them. And the old pros are staying home."

"That's what it looks like," he said.

"Where is the meat?" John asked.

"They got it in their deep-freezes," his source continued. "John, I've got something else to tell you."

"What's that?"

"Martin Gill owns a meat-saw. He's been sawing up the meat for the boys. Instead of them paying him, they're giving him moose meat. And, my son, he has a deep-freeze that's full, right to the cover! Now I'm going to tell you where it is." With that, he outlined the entire situation to the officer.

"Now, John," he said as he finished, "you've got the whole story. The rest is up to you. You know which houses to search, and I wish you luck. Goodbye."

John had most of the details before him on paper. He reviewed them, and, satisfied with the report, he called Norman Muise. He would not tell him anything on the phone. Instead, he arranged a meeting before noon for the following day at Hawke's Bay. He agreed.

He called Eric Kinden and their temporary game warden, Donald Gillard, for a meeting right away, to brief them and discuss their options before meeting Norman Muise in the morning.

John met with Norman the following day and briefed him on what he had found out. They double-checked everything, and were satisfied they had enough information to give them reasonable cause to conduct searches. They secured the assistance of the

R.C.M.P. from the Roddickton Detachment, brought in wildlife officers from the Stephenville, Corner Brook and Deer Lake areas, and made their plans.

With two helicopters and Rex Boyd's Cessna 185, they moved in on Cat Cove just before noon. Conducting searches in the two sections of the town, they found meat in every house except Mary Pollard's.

The surprising thing was that the fellows who had hunted and shot the moose didn't get charged, but their parents did. One of the parents was Joseph Gill. They charged him with illegal possession of moose meat in closed season. He pleaded guilty.

The offenders appeared in court at Roddickton and were convicted. They received large fines and an embarrassing lecture from the judge. However, the wildlife officers remained unsatisfied because they hadn't caught the people who had done the actual shooting. But they knew there would be another time.

When Joseph Gill stood in court with Pollard, the officers made sure the court was aware that it was Gill's second wildlife charge. The officers pointed out the extent of the slaughter of moose in the area that was evident around that time, and insisted that something would definitely have to be done to discourage it. They suggested that heavy sentences would send a message to poachers. The judge took this information into consideration and gave Joseph Gill a $3,000.00 fine and a thirty-day jail sentence. In addition to forfeiting his gun and snowmobile, he was prohibited from holding a big game licence for five years.

Chapter 4

Ryland Gill's Secret Cache

During April of 1985, Officer Christian was working in the Cat Cove/Hawke's Bay area, and staying in the wildlife patrol cabin. He was watching a small caribou herd nearby.

One day, he decided to make a patrol out to Cat Cove. On the way, he noticed that foxes had been digging under his trail. Of course, he began to wonder why they were doing that, so he stopped his snowmobile to investigate.

After digging a little into the snow, to his surprise he discovered moose hair and blood. Then he realized what was going on. Someone had buried moose meat under his trail, and he had been driving over it with no suspicion it was even there!

"Well, well!" he said. "This looks very interesting. I've got to investigate this further."

Kneeling down, he examined the blood and hair, then smelled the blood to determine how fresh it was. He estimated it had been put there around the first of February, approximately two months earlier.

33

He started his machine and continued his patrol to Cat Cove. He thought, *I bet that's the same moose that was killed on the fifth or sixth of February past, most likely on the fifth. If only I had something to go on.*

He thought it looked like the work of Ryland Gill. *Yes, maybe it was him,* he mused. *It's possible I'm on the right track after all.* But, he still knew this would be a hard case to crack.

He arrived at Cat Cove and took a run around the town, checking a few sheds and watching for places where the local dogs were digging around trees or snowbanks. This is how he often succeeded in finding meat buried around towns or along trails.

He dropped into a home for a cup of tea. The people welcomed him, and his host told him about another game warden who had come into town one afternoon a couple of weeks before. There was a wedding that night, and most of the residents had a moose roast cooking for the big supper scoff.

Suddenly, there had been a hue and cry that John Christian was in town. Most of the people dumped their roasts immediately. Others carried their roasters into the woods and hid them.

But when it was learned that the game warden in town wasn't John Christian, everything returned to normal. The roasting of illegal meat continued, in preparation for the wedding feast.

"John," the man of the house said to him, "if you had come that time, you would have broken up a wedding!"

They had a great laugh. Then they had a lunch.

After they ate, John said, "I saw a funny thing on my way out here this afternoon."

"What was that?" the man asked.

"I discovered there was moose meat under my trail, and the foxes had it dug up."

The man had quite a laugh for himself. John waited eagerly to hear what he was going to say.

"John, boy," he said, "this has been the big laugh on you this winter!"

"Why?"

"Well, when the partridge season opened on the fifth of February, Ryland Gill and Carl Manuel, the boyfriend of the woman who rented Ryland Gill's basement, went in on the right-of-way, and knocked down a big bull on the brook. They killed him with shot. Nobody knows how many times they fired at him before they brought him down. Then they just cut his throat and ran.

"The next day, a couple of people from here went in that way for a ride—and there was Mr. Ryland sitting down and having a beer right in the light of noonday, while Carl and another fellow from here were quartering the moose. Then they took the meat and buried it under your trail. During every snowstorm, they would go in and bring out so much.

"You don't mean it!" John exclaimed.

"Yes, I do," he said. "And every time you came out here, they would say, 'Boy, John came out over the moose again!' Then they would have a big laugh about it!"

John thought for a moment. "You never know, friend, you never know."

"John, Ryland has to be caught. Last year he killed about thirty-four moose, and I'd say he's close to that number again this year. I don't know how you didn't nail him last year. Certainly, I guess he bought his way out of it, and now he's laughing at you. And I'd say he'll get away with this one, too!"

John looked at him and spoke with determination. "We'll see, sir! We'll see about that!"

The incident in which Ryland had escaped charges happened in January, 1984. One day, while on patrol, John had caught six people with two moose hooked to their snowmobiles. They were on their way out to Cat Cove. There was a blizzard on at the time.

Ryland Gill was one of the men, but because he wasn't pulling the meat, he said he was only travelling with the other men in the group. Another man pleaded guilty. The judge let Ryland off on a plea bargain for good conduct, then gave the other men a thousand-dollar fine each, forfeiting their three Ski-doos to the Crown, and forfeiting the possibility of a big game licence for five years.

The officer's informant friend knew all about this incident, but he didn't know that John had excellent evidence stored at home, or that all he needed now was the actual shotgun. He knew where he had to look for it—where else but at Ryland Gill's house?

After chatting awhile longer, John thanked him for the lunch and left his house.

Chapter 5

Stakeout Near Cat Cove

On May 15, 1985, John Christian left his home at Roddickton and went to Corner Brook to attend a meeting with the Crown Attorney, David King. In the afternoon, he met with Clarence Maloney and discussed with him the problem he was having with poaching in his area. They decided on a few strategies to handle some of the problems.

Following the meeting, he checked into Corner Brook's Mamateek Inn on the Trans Canada Highway, where he stayed for the night. He didn't immediately contact his wife to let her know where he was staying, as he usually did when he was away from home. She finally tracked him down at around 10:00 p.m. It was urgent; she had an important telephone message.

Someone from Cat Cove had called her with the information that there were two men in the woods hunting moose, and that they had killed an animal. It was a good chance that one of them was Ryland Gill. The person requested that John go to Cat Cove without delay.

Cat Cove is an isolated community, and the only way there during the summer is by boat or airplane and, during the winter, by snowmobile or airplane. It was too late for him to go that night.

He called Clarence Maloney and gave him all the information he had received. It was late, and Maloney said he was unable to do anything about the situation until 9:00 a.m. They talked about the cost involved, but each of them knew this was an emergency. If they were to catch Ryland Gill, this could be their chance. Regardless of the expenses, they would consider the money to be well-spent if they could get a charge laid against the man and stop his poaching activity.

At eight-thirty the next morning, John met Clarence at their Pasadena office. They held a short meeting, and decided to obtain a helicopter and go to Cat Cove to investigate. Calling Universal Helicopters, they arranged to have a Jet Ranger at their disposal. Their pilot was none other than John Ennis. With twenty years of experience in helicopter flying, Ennis had done much work in chasing poachers and was very successful at this type of work. Always doing the right thing at the right time, he had the advantage of knowing the Great Northern Peninsula like a book.

At nine, Randy Trask, the law enforcement officer stationed at Pasadena, came to the office. An able man, he too knew his field well and could take the rough going, which was vitally important in his type of work. Randy would become the wildlife enforcement supervisor for Gander.

They briefed Randy on what was happening, after which Clarence assigned him to work with Christian on the case. Randy was delighted to be part of the operation.

They put together their gear, including snowshoes, sleeping bags, a tent, tarpaulin, stove, lantern, flashlight, rope, clipboard, camera, writing material, food and cooking utensils.

Going to the hangar, they met John Ennis. They briefed him, giving him the details of what they planned to do. Once they arrived at the spot where the kill supposedly took place, they wanted to confirm the report they had received. If it were positive, they would then decide what to do. They had to be careful not to alert anyone in Cat Cove.

At 11:00 a.m. they left Pasadena. It was a beautiful, clear, sunny late-spring day with not a breath of wind in the air. Flying over the open country, they could see scattered moose and caribou on the move. From the air, it seemed that snowmobiling conditions from Pasadena to Cat Cove were fair. The helicopter ride usually took fifty minutes, but they made it in half an hour.

As they entered the Cat Cove area, John Christian could see in the distance snowmobile tracks leading into the area where the slaughter had evidently taken place. The tracks came up to a small pond not far ahead of them.

He said to the pilot, "Be careful not to let anyone see you. Keep as low as possible."

"Okay, John."

Ennis flew low enough for the helicopter to hug the treetops as they circled.

"There's a kill here for sure!" Christian said. "Look at the crows! Look there! See that eagle?"

"Something's here for sure," Randy Trask said.

"There are moose tracks," Ennis said as he manoeuvred the chopper. "The boys must have it in among the trees."

"You're right," John said. "I think that's where they've got it."

As they continued circling, John motioned for Ennis to keep his craft to the left.

"Hey!" Christian shouted. "Look! There's a kill!" He had spotted a dead moose that had recently been slit open.

"Okay," he said to the pilot, "let's put her down on the back there."

They saw a small pond about a hundred yards back from the kill. The pilot quickly manoeuvred the helicopter low, dropping it gently to the pond.

Randy Trask and John Christian climbed out of the helicopter. They decided what to do first. They told the pilot they were going to check the kill and begin their investigation.

Christian said to the pilot, "You might as well shut down the machine. This could probably take quite awhile."

"Well, then," Ennis said, "I might as well join you."

"Good," they said in unison. "Let's go."

They put on their snowshoes. At this time of the day, the snow was soft; they knew they were going to have difficulty travelling, even with snowshoes.

They were about three miles west of Cat Cove. The area where the kill took place was located between two ponds on the side of a small ridge at the edge of a cutover. The rest of the area was heavily wooded. There was also a small brook at the base of the ridge. This brook ran out of the pond where they had landed their helicopter.

Trask and Christian walked slowly through the trees, carefully picking their steps. They made sure that, if any people came into the area to get the meat, they wouldn't be alerted to the officers' presence by their tracks.

40

They walked over to the kill and examined it. The animal, a large cow, was slit open and its paunch was pulled out. By the signs around the place, it appeared to have been a fast job. They also examined the snowshoe tracks of the people who had killed the moose. One set of tracks was sinking into the snow more than the other.

These signs indicated that the men were Ryland Gill, a heavily-built man, and Luke Greene, a slighter-built man, weighting about 140 pounds. From their observations they established that only two men were involved.

They saw where the poachers had come to within a hundred feet of the kill, apparently using only one snowmobile. They shot the cow, slit it open, and left, taking nothing with them. The officers found a pair of new, white nylon gloves near the paunch. Now they were sure this was the work of Ryland Gill. Nobody else in Cat Cove could afford to leave a pair of gloves like these at the site of the kill. Also, this appeared to be one of his latest habits—using a pair of white nylon gloves, and leaving them behind after the kill.

"Okay," Christian said, "I feel sure there won't be anyone here today. It's too risky on a day like this for them to come after the meat. What we will do now is to go on to Roddickton to get some more equipment." Before leaving their office at Pasadena, he had prepared warrants to search the homes of Ryland Gill and Luke Greene at Cat Cove. He knew these wouldn't be of any use the next day. "That means we'll have to get more warrants made up," he said.

All of them agreed to come back late in the afternoon. Returning to the helicopter, they put on their headphones while John Ennis started the engine.

"What do you think, boys?" Christian asked. "Hey, Randy! What do you think?"

"Well," Randy said, "your report certainly was a good one, that's for sure! But why do you think they shot that moose and just left it? It sure looks kind of strange to me. They just dropped that cow, pulled out her paunch, and ran. They never hung around at all."

"I don't know," Christian answered slowly.

"Boy, oh boy!" Ennis said. "What a crime! Can you imagine shooting that cow at this time of the year, on the fifteenth of May?"

Turning to Christian, Randy asked, "What do *you* think, John?"

"There's one thing for sure," he said. "It's going to be hard to convict them unless we catch them right in the act. We have enough evidence now to use our search warrants, but what's the use of searching when they haven't taken any of the meat out yet? I'd say they're guaranteed to be back after the meat when it gets dark, or sometime later tonight anyway."

"You're probably right," Randy said.

"We should take some of this gear out of the helicopter, if it's okay with you," Christian said to the pilot.

"Yes, that's a good idea," Ennis agreed. "It'll lighten us up quite a bit."

The two officers jumped out, removed some of their gear, and stashed it in the woods. Then they climbed back in the helicopter and took off, flying just above the treetops.

As they flew inland, John Christian told the others what he considered to be the best thing to do at the moment. "We've got to have a stakeout," he said. "As I see it, that would be the best way to catch these

42

men. Right now we'll go on to Roddickton, and you can drop me off there. Then you can go on to St. Anthony and refuel."

St. Anthony is situated on the tip of the Great Northern Peninsula. "While you're gone," he continued, "I'll get a few more things together, and phone Clarence."

"Okay," they said.

Within thirty-five minutes they were at Roddickton. John got out near his home, and Randy and the pilot left for St. Anthony. He went to the R.C.M.P. Detachment, had the required search warrants prepared, then went to the Justice of the Peace and had the warrants sworn to.

Chapter 6

Blood on the Hills

At 3:30 p.m., the helicopter returned and picked up John Christian at a secret place on the outskirts of the town. They headed back to Cat Cove via the Doctor's Hills, a Range of mountains located on the west side of the Great Northern Peninsula.

This was a good caribou range, but poaching had all but wiped out the herd in the area. The caribou that went there belonged to the Williamsport herd, and not many of them came back. The poachers got most of the animals as soon as they reached the area. In fact, just a couple of weeks before, on a routine wildlife patrol in the same area, Officer Christian had taken some pictures of an unborn calf he had cut from a caribou paunch.

When their eyes caught sight of snowmobile tracks in the caribou range, John was certain they were there for only one reason. "They were made by poachers!" They kept watching for anything that looked suspicious.

"Hey, fellows!" he exclaimed. "Look at this! See the blood? Just look over there! There's blood on the hills!"

John Ennis quickly manoeuvred the helicopter around and dropped lower so they could have a closer look at the area.

"Look over there!" Randy instructed, pointing to low brush on the side of a pond. "It looks like they've got it buried there."

"Maybe you're right," Christian said.

He turned to the pilot. "John, can you put her down near that area?"

"Sure I can," he said. "No problem." He adeptly lowered the craft.

Getting out of the helicopter, they walked over to the area where they had seen the blood. They could see two caribou heads and eight legs. It was obvious what had happened. The poachers had come upon the caribou farther back, killed the animals and paunched them, pulling the carcasses out to this area. Here they cut them up, loaded them on sleighs and carried them home. Perhaps they waited until midnight to haul out the quarters, or they might have buried them in the snow farther out toward Castors River.

The river's headwaters are in the slopes of the Long Range Mountains; the river itself flows west 60 kilometres (40 miles) across the Great Northern Peninsula to its mouth in St. John Bay.

Rechecking what they thought had happened, they went back to the helicopter to brief the pilot. They asked him if he could go out toward Castors River to check along the trail.

"I certainly can," he assured them. "Gladly! John, what in the world are they trying to do? Kill everything in the country? I've never seen the likes before!"

45

"It's almost like trying to catch ghosts!" Ennis exclaimed.

"You're right, there!" Randy said.

They took to the air again, deciding to follow the snowmobile tracks for awhile. A mile or so later, they saw below them three men on snowmobiles coming toward them on the open country. They were inside the treeline about half a mile.

"Now," Christian said to the pilot, "you know what you have to do to stop them. Make sure we catch them all!"

"Okay." Experienced in stopping poachers, John Ennis put his knowledge to good use without delay. He moved in on the lead guy, and before the man knew what was happening, had the Jet Ranger sitting directly in front of him! Randy bolted from the craft like a German Shepherd and took the man into custody.

The helicopter lifted off again, and they moved on to the next man. They stopped him. John Christian got out quickly and arrested him. The third man stopped where he was.

They checked three of them. They were carrying slugs and a shotgun. The caribou herd was down to twenty-six animals, nearly extinct, and at the last sentencing involving caribou poaching the judge promised to impose harsh sentences if it happened again. These men were well aware of this and were scared to be charged with poaching caribou. They did, however, give the officers a statement, making it clear they were poaching moose only.

They searched the men and seized their snowmobiles. They were cautioned and read their rights. When their investigation was completed, John

Ennis and Officer Christian flew them out to Castors River. Next, they went back, picked up Randy and continued on toward Cat Cove.

The three men they had arrested appeared later in court at Port au Choix, on the northwest coast of the Great Northern Peninsula, where they were convicted of hunting big game. Each of them received a thousand dollar fine. They were prohibited from holding a big game licence for five years and, in default of payment of their fines, were to spend thirty days in jail. They favoured the latter option.

Randy and John Christian arrived at the drop-off point near the moose kill they were investigating. They asked the pilot to contact Clarence Maloney and arrange to have three men go to the Doctor's Hills area to drive out the three Ski-doos they had seized. They also asked him to return at ten the next morning. Agreeing, he left.

They were now in total silence, except for the screeching sound of a Canadian Jay and the loud caw of a crow as it was driven away from its meal of fresh meat. They put on their snowshoes, and loaded down with gear, walked to the area where the moose were killed.

They surveyed the area, being careful to avoid the trail or any spot where someone coming in for the meat would be alerted. Then they found a perfect place to set up their tent, after which they decided to locate an outpost. To do this, Officer Christian put his army training into practice.

In December, 1960, John enlisted in the Canadian Army, serving with the Princess Patricia's Canadian

Light Infantry. He took his basic training in Wainwright, Alberta. That winter was one of severe blizzards. However, the fact that he came from a winter logging area meant he was familiar with such conditions, and he had no problems with his training. In fact, he loved every minute of it!

After finishing training, he was posted to Victoria, British Columbia, where he met Sergeant Courteaur, who became their Company Sergeant. After being at Work Point Barracks a short time, they were told that Sergeant Courteaur had been Canada's most decorated soldier during World War II. He came from Saskatchewan. A remarkable man, he picked John to work with his platoon whenever they went on manoeuvres. He remembered Courteaur telling him, "Newf, if you ever decide to do something, don't start it unless you intend to finish it, because the only ones who contributed anything to our nation were the ones who started and finished."

John often said that everything his sergeant taught him when under his watchful eye were things he had to use since beginning to work as an enforcement officer with the Department of Wildlife. Because of the tricks he taught him, many poachers had been caught. He knew his army training would help him in the present situation.

Their outpost was set up in such a way that they would stay hidden, yet would be able to see anything that came their way. They also made sure they would be able to corner anyone coming back from the location of the moose. In order to secure good evidence for court, they knew they would have to make sure the person had actually handled the meat.

Sitting in their orange-coloured tent, they heard an airplane flying overhead. They were really concerned, because they knew Ryland Gill's brother-in-law had a small plane. Maybe he had decided to take a look at the moose, and even look for more animals to kill.

John ran to the tent, pulled the corner strings and let the structure fall down. He quickly cut some boughs and covered the tent, camouflaging it. Now there was no way for the people in the plane to see the tent from the air. They could breathe easier. To his surprise, the plane flew over them and continued in a northerly direction. This assured them it wasn't from Cat Cove.

They went back to the moose kill. Looking around the area, they noticed the tracks the animal had made; it had evidently been floundering around in the deep, soft snow. They also observed that two or three more moose had escaped over the side of the hill on which they were standing. Further investigation near the kill revealed that the hot sun had melted much of the snow.

They looked for empty bullet casings, their experience in the field paying off. If an empty bullet casing is dropped in the snow, and the sun is allowed to shine on it, it becomes warm quickly because of its hollow body. It then sinks fast on its side. Because the burnt powder turns black, the casing can be seen easily in the snow. They found two spent shells of 30-30 calibre, and filed them as Exhibit #3.

They made a second outpost near the moose. Moving from one outpost to another would help to break up the time. The weather was getting colder, reaching the freezing point by sunset.

Putting the kettle on the stove to boil the water, John prepared dinner. He put a piece of meat—not

49

moose!—in a pan for Randy, who was in the other outpost. When the meat was heated on one side, he turned it over and warmed the other side. Then he called Randy inside.

He looked at the meat. "John," he exclaimed, "that meat isn't even fried! It's still bleeding!"

"You're not under your mother's care now!" Christian said. "I'll put it this way: Anyone who can't eat that meat has no business being in here!"

Randy laughed. "You're right, ol' man! You're right!" He picked up the piece of meat in his hands and devoured it.

After dinner, both men went to the second outpost. Darkness soon fell and, at one point, Randy thought he heard someone approaching. He insisted he could hear a Ski-doo engine, and scolded his partner for being hard of hearing, only to admit later it had been a false alarm. John had been out on numerous other stakeouts when men claimed to hear and see things during the night, only to say later they *thought* they did!

Two or three hours passed quickly as John entertained Randy about a book he had just finished reading. Entitled *Assault Norway,* it told the story of a Norwegian commando crew that blew up the German heavy water plant near Oslo during World War II.

He told Randy about his amateur boxing career, describing some of the most exciting moments when he had won several titles. Randy had done some boxing himself; they had no trouble exchanging comments about the sport.

They discussed poaching, and how difficult it was to get the public to realize that poachers were stopping them from obtaining licences to hunt big game in season. John told Randy about many of the cases he had worked on over the years. "You know, Randy," he said, "this sort of reminds me of an incident that happened awhile back when I was on a stakeout."

A stakeout is a peculiar job, requiring great patience, because it involves plenty of waiting around for something to happen. He described a couple of the cases in detail. One of them was particularly vivid.

Chapter 7

The Soufflets River Chase

B ob Way and John Christian worked at home in Roddickton on February 7, 1985. There had been a heavy snowfall after a bad storm. Poaching was totally out of control. Fellows refused to accept the fact that officers were out on the hills, enforcing the wildlife laws. Their presence didn't seem to slow down their poaching activities at all.

When Bob and John left for the Soufflets River area on a patrol, they took their gear and started up Cloud River, breaking their way through the deep snow. Some fellows were rabbit-catching by the officers' cabin on the upper part of the river. John knew they would have the road broken in, so they punched their way along. As they suspected, they came to the tracks of the men about twenty miles in from Roddickton, and proceeded to the camp.

It was well past noon when they reached the cabin. There were three men there: Enos Gillard and his two sons, Ralph and Don. They were doing quite well rabbit-catching.

Don, who was about thirty-five years old, decided to join the officers on their patrol. They were pleased he wanted to accompany them, because breaking snow was hard work, and they needed all of the help they could get.

They ate lunch at the cabin, which was actually a Wildlife cabin. Don took his snowmobile, and the three of them left. It wasn't a good evening, but the weather was beginning to clear, and it looked like things would be better later on.

They had to use a compass when they reached the top of the country, where there was nothing but eighteen miles of flat, open land. They followed a compass course, and steered across until they struck the Green Diamond Skirt. Then they went out to Rocky Stent, and started up Soufflets River Valley.

They were heading for their cabin, approximately three or four miles up the valley, when suddenly, they saw the tracks of three snowmobiles. It seemed they had come over from Port au Choix, crossed the bogs and headed for the Soufflets River area.

The partridge season had opened a couple of days before. "Listen here," John said to the others. "Do you know that those fellows gone in there are up to no good?"

Naturally, his companions wanted to know why he thought that way.

He pointed to the tracks, which were moving around the trees and skirting bunches of woods. The drivers were in areas along the river where they shouldn't have been. He checked there, then came back.

"Okay, now," he said. "This is what we're going to do. I'm going to gas up my snowmobile. You fellows can go on to the cabin and get it dug out, get some wood, and do whatever else needs to be done there."

Bob Way and Don Gillard were the kind of fellows who never had to be told what to do. They were excellent men to work with.

"I'll go on the tracks of these fellows," John said. "For sure, they're out there somewhere." The suspects hadn't crossed their trail; they would have seen the tracks had they done so. Also, in order for them to come up out of the area where they had gone, the officers would have seen them.

Bob and Don went on to the cabin, hauling the sleighs containing the wildlife gear. John got on the tracks of the three Ski-doos and continued down the brook, following in their tracks. He was sure these men were poachers, because they were skirting areas frequented by moose.

John continued down the valley, tracking the suspects. Their movements indicated they would go down, then come back so far, and head through patches of woods. The tracks turned in the direction of Red Sea Pond, heading toward Williamsport. They skirted the entire area, as well as all of the stands of woods, before heading back across the countryside toward Port au Choix.

John followed them until they arrived back at his tracks and crossed over them. However, it seemed to him that they hadn't noticed the tracks. Their oversight was to his advantage. Probably because it was so blind travelling on the open country, with its whiteouts, they were unable to see the tracks even as they crossed them.

Taking their original track, he headed up the valley to their camp and stopped where the boys were. Bob Way had a supper cooking—salt beef, potatoes, turnip and cabbage.

As he sat down, John said, "Boys, listen! I've got a feeling that there's hunting going on up here in this valley. Now I'll tell you what I'm going to do. While supper's cooking, I'll take a run up the valley and have a good look around."

The others were kept busy, getting things organized in the brand-new sturdy cabin, built from matched lumber the previous fall. While they were doing their work, John gassed up his snowmobile again, and started up the valley.

He went across the pond and over the barrens. By now the weather had cleared, and it was a beautiful evening. There was no wind, the sky was blue, and the sun was just beginning to disappear behind the hills.

Reaching the top of the hill, he continued along, keeping his eyes open for anything that looked suspicious. He picked up three sets of snowmobile tracks, stopped and looked at them. *Mmmm,* he said to himself, *these look like the same three tracks I've been following all evening.*

He could easily figure out what these fellows had done. They had come back and gone around the area of their camp, being careful not to come in too close to it. He guessed that they had guns and rifles, and didn't want to be seen. Since they were unsure if anyone was in the camp, they decided to stay out of sight. They went behind the mountains, then swung around to circle the head of the valley.

They reached the same hill Officer Christian was on, and looked out through the valley. Because Bob and Don hadn't arrived yet, there were no tracks to be seen on the pond. As far as the suspects were concerned, everything was fine.

"Let's go, boys!" they must have said to each other.

They got on the track of some caribou right on the hill, and went down into the valley toward the west, moving farther away from the camp. Then they started to hunt the caribou in the valley, where, apparently, the animals had been there the day before, coming off the barrens, going down into the valley to feed. Then they went back to the barrens, located two or three miles farther west. Now these fellows were after the caribou, and John wasn't far behind them.

He tracked them down in the valley, went to the pond inside it, crossed the falls, then returned from the valley. Coming up out of the valley toward the east, he saw where they turned onto a barren before heading into the high country again.

He suddenly saw caribou tracks, then caribou running. And what a sight that greeted him! Caribou heads, legs and paunches were lying all over the place. He went closer.

"Well, boys," he said, "you've sure killed a whole slew of caribou!"

He reconstructed what they had done. They shot the caribou out on the open country, then used their snowmobiles to tow them to this spot before cleaning them. Looking around, John saw a dozen or so trees growing in a little nook, like they often did on the side of the country. He noticed where the tracks went in through the trees. He looked in through the opening and saw the caribou quarters. The men had quartered all of the caribou they had killed, and stacked the pieces like cords of wood.

He looked around and sized up the situation, trying to figure out what their plans were. If these fellows had planned to come back here in a day or so, or after a snowstorm—as poachers usually did—they would have dug a hole and put the caribou in it. Then they would have thrown boughs over it, and piled snow on top of the boughs to keep the crows from eating the meat.

Because the meat was laid out in the open, he figured they must have planned to return after dark that night to get it. He had learned that this was how the poachers operated.

They would make a fast run on the high, open country, knock down a few caribou, remove the gut, and race off the highlands. They were scared of being seen by wildlife on their helicopter patrols. Soon after it got dark, or sometimes very late at night, they would come back and recover the meat.

John continued to think over the situation and mused aloud, "Around eight tonight, they're going to be coming back for this meat. They won't want to give anyone a chance to find and steal what they have hidden. That means we're going to have to hide somewhere around here in order to catch them."

He looked around for a good hiding place. There was a twenty-foot rise about a hundred feet from where the meat was stacked. Up there, he noticed, was a place where they could hide behind some trees under a little hill, thereby providing shelter from anybody coming in from the open country. A deep crevice in front also blocked anybody who might approach from that direction. Poachers would not see their snowmobiles when they came to get the meat. All things considered, he thought it was an ideal hiding place.

John decided to go back and get the boys, knowing he had to make a move before it got too dark. They had to be prepared early because they would not be able to turn on their lights, in case someone might be coming down the country before dark.

He went back down the valley, heading to the Wildlife cabin. It was dark by the time he got there. He bolted inside.

"Boys!" he said. "Listen! There's been an awful slaughter up there on the country! Now this is what we've got to do. We've got to play our cards right if we want to catch the ones who are guilty of doing this. We've got to go up there and hide away by the meat. I think they'll be back for it sometime after eight tonight, and we have to be there before then, stowed away." He also explained why he expected the men to return for the meat later that night.

"Okay!" he continued. "We've got no time to lose, so make sure your snowmobiles are gassed up. Don, fill a five-gallon can with gas. We'll need it if we have to go on a chase."

In the meantime, Bob and Don had a big, hot supper cooked, and the utensils on the table, just waiting for John to return before supper was served. Now, however, there was no time to eat. They left everything, put on their clothes, took a sleigh, and jumped on their snowmobiles.

"Listen, boys," he told them. "Don't put your headlights on, and be sure to stay on my track. Don't leave my track for any reason whatsoever. I'm going to get geared up now, get all the stuff I need, so you fellows go on ahead, but remember—no headlights, and stay on my track!"

After they left, he grabbed a bite of the food. *I think I should take my sleeping bag,* he told himself, *just in case. You never know, I might need it.*

He took his heavy sleeping bag and tied it to his sleigh before heading out. He hadn't gone very far before he met the boys coming back to the cabin.

"Boy, oh boy!" one of them said. "John, we can't follow your tracks, my son! It's impossible! It's too dark to see them!"

"Okay, then. Now, listen! Get behind me!"

They got behind him, keeping on his track going down in the valley. He took his time, kept checking his watch, and turned up where the kills were. He went straight up around, then in over the bank. When they finally reached their hiding place, everything was secured. In over the bank, they used their flashlights and got everything settled away. It was now around 6:45 p.m.

"The lads are going to be here by eight," he said. "Guaranteed! I know how these fellas usually operate. They would have waited until about ten minutes before six to leave for here. This time of the year, it is beginning to get dark by then, so they should already be on their way in. They're going to be taking their time coming on up through. It's going to take them the best part of two hours to get in here from where they are. They will be pretty cautious coming through the woods here as they get near to the meat, don't worry!

"Here's what we'll do while we're waiting. Every fifteen minutes or so, we'll start up our machines to make sure they're running okay."

That was exactly what they did. The snowmobiles weren't like the ones Wildlife has today. The lights didn't come on automatically when the machines were started. They had to be switched on manually, so they had no worries about their lights coming on and signaling their whereabouts to poachers.

While they were waiting, they got into a conversation.

"Boys," John said, "if they are the fellows I'm thinking about, they have a revolver." He had to tell his companions this, because he didn't want them to think they were kidding around.

"Don," he continued, "you stay here. Don't go out and get involved. Bob will go with me, and if anything happens—like the both of us getting shot—you can tell the tale!" He was joking, but Bob got somewhat nervous.

"Now look here!" Bob said. "This isn't fit to be at! John, what in the world are we doing in here, my son?"

John looked at Bob, noticing he was wearing only a light jacket. He didn't have his heavy coat with him, so John took his sleeping bag and wrapped it around him. It was good he had decided to bring it.

They remained where they were, passing the time and talking about different things. They waited and waited. Seven o'clock, seven-fifteen, seven-thirty. Still nobody showed up.

"Listen!" Bob said. "Let's go now. Why don't we take the meat and go on back to the camp?"

"No sirree!" John answered. "We're here now, and we're staying here until something happens!"

Seven-forty-five arrived. "Boys!" he said. "Look down the country." They looked down as far as they could see.

"Look!" he said. "One light, two lights, three lights! Here they come!"

The fellows hadn't been involved in anything like this before, and they were really nervous. "Now boys," John said, "listen! When they get down here, whatever you do, keep out of sight! Let them come right on in where the meat is, and make sure they start loading it before you make a move. Whatever you do, don't make a move until then! You'd better remember that, because it's very important."

The snowmobiles came on down, their drivers completely unaware that three others were peering over the snowbank, watching them. They headed straight in their direction, and were just a few feet from them, when suddenly, they had to stop because of a deep crevice.

"Boys!" one of the men said. "'Tis around here. This is the place right along here somewhere."

They looked around the area. One fellow called out, "Hey! There it is! I can see the blood! This is where we killed them all right! Right over here!"

The other two fellows joined him, and the three of them circled around on their snowmobiles. They came out and stopped right where the meat was lying. The drivers shut off their lights, which had been shining directly toward the officers. They watched the suspects, listening carefully.

One of the suspects said, "You know, boys, it looks like someone was here since we were here last."

The others laughed. "Go on!" one of them said. "Don't be so silly! That's our tracks you're looking at!"

The trio seemed to relax after that, and began to laugh and talk. They got their flashlights, and started in loading the meat.

In the stakeout hideaway, John began issuing instructions. "Now boys, listen! We'll all put our hands on our starters. Understand?"

The three of them gripped their throttles.

"Bob," he continued, "when I say 'lights,' you turn on your lights, okay?"

He waited a few seconds, then issued the order. "Okay Bob. Your lights!"

Bob's light came on, but John's own machine refused to start! He hauled on the starter. Not a sound! He pulled again, but the machine still didn't start.

He jumped up. "Bob," he cried. "Get 'em!"

"Not me!" Bob said.

John jumped out and ran for the machines. On came three lights, and out came the Ski-doos, going full tilt.

"Bob," he shouted again. "Get 'em."

"No!" he declared. "I'm not, sir!"

Two of the fellows passed John, and the third was on his way out. John got down and watched him approaching. John was blocking his path, so he pulled his machine toward him. Bob leaped toward him, but the machine swept by. He kept coming full speed toward Christian, who had to jump to one side to avoid being run over and killed; the impact of the machine's bumper knocked him sideways, but as it flew by he grabbed the driver by the head.

The driver gripped the handlebars with one hand clamped down on the throttle, revving the engine to a roar. He had a sleigh in tow, and to dodge its nose John had to keep hopping, while at the same time keeping a tight grip on the driver. He finally managed to tear away, leaving John behind, holding the man's cap. Bareheaded, the driver sped off, full throttle ahead.

John turned around. "Go get 'em, Bob!" he said. "Stop 'em, boy!"

He bawked once again. "No way, sir! Not me!"

He couldn't blame Bob for feeling that way, because these poachers were reckless and dangerous.

He ran back to his snowmobile, took out his flashlight, and looked the machine over. He noticed that the "kill" button was pushed in. He pushed up on it and, putting it in the "on" position, hauled to start the engine. The pull cord stayed out, and the machine refused to start. He had to take out his wrenches, take the starter apart, and put it back together again. This was done in short order and he was ready to go again.

He spoke to the boys, "You go back and hook up the sleigh we left way back on the trail. Take the can of gasoline, and then come on up and get on my tracks and follow me, because I'm leaving right now."

They left to go get the sleigh, as requested. Getting on the tracks of the three suspects, John was travelling as fast as the snowmobile could go. Suddenly, he went over a large, flat rock. He found himself in mid-air, and then landed with a thump on another rock.

Clearing his head, he caught sight of a beat-up snowmobile with a bent ski. It wasn't his own. Looking around, he figured out what had happened. The suspect who owned that machine had gone over the same rock, and beat up his machine. He then jumped aboard a sleigh behind another snowmobile. John could see where the two remaining machines separated, each going in a different direction.

He decided to get on the track of the machine that was towing the sleigh. It was amazing, seeing where these men went as he chased them over the steep barrens on the country. One fellow would get off to walk up the inclines because they were so steep and slippery; the other fellow would then haul his companion up over the hills.

When John got up on the country, he looked down. In the distance, he saw the taillight of a snowmobile. It was gradually moving away from him, and he knew these were the men he was after.

Looking at the machine ahead of him, he was reminded of a fox hunt where the dogs go after the animals and hunt them down. Here he was, with a 440, high-horsepowered snowmobile. He had no sleigh in tow, and he was chasing fellows with a small Ski-doo of about sixteen horsepower. That machine was towing a sleigh, which carried a man.

It didn't take him long to catch up with them. He noticed that the man on the sleigh was lying on his stomach. *Boy!* he thought, *You've had a rough ride!*

The country was really rugged, and the men were moving at full speed.

John pulled alongside. "Stop!" he called. The driver didn't even notice him. He moved closer to his quarry and called out louder, "Stop, sir! Stop!"

He still didn't slacken his speed. John knew he had to take further action. He moved out about fifteen feet, then came in and rammed the side of the other snowmobile with the side of his own. Still the driver refused to stop. He just straightened up his machine and sped on.

"So, you're not going to stop her, eh?" John said.

The driver didn't speak, but continued to stare straight ahead. The man on the sleigh was silent, too. John raced ahead a hundred or so yards, turned around, and came full speed toward the other snowmobile. *Buddy, we'll see who's got the most nerve now!*

Seeing the headlight dull on the other machine, he knew it was stopping. Christian slackened his speed, applied his brakes and stopped his machine next to the other. He locked his ski with the other so the driver couldn't move his vehicle. John got off his machine.

"Okay, boys," he said. "You're under suspicion of killing caribou."

"We don't know anything about any caribou being killed," they said almost in unison.

"No?" John countered. "Well, you're under suspicion, and I'm placing you under arrest."

He cautioned them, placing them under arrest. He took their axe and questioned them, asking if they knew anything about the caribou that had been killed. They denied everything.

"Okay," he said to them, "then I'm taking you back to the camp."

He ran a line from his snowmobile to the other, took it in tow, and started back to the camp. He soon met his two buddies, who had caught up with him.

"All right, boys," he said, "you go on ahead and pick up all our gear, and start hauling the meat over to the camp."

They left immediately. John went on with the fellows he had arrested, heading for the camp.

At the camp, he checked the stove. There were still some hot coals there, so he threw some gasoline over the wood he had tossed in the stove. What an explosion when he dropped in a match! The two men with him weren't the type to be easily frightened, but what a look came on their faces!

John also got an awful start.

Bob and Don showed up, and they had supper. The prisoners still wouldn't tell them anything about what had happened, who had helped them, or who the third man was. John later realized that he was lucky to catch these men while using his machine, which wasn't working properly at the time. They stayed at the cabin for the night.

The next morning, they got up at about four o'clock.

"Listen, you fellows," John said to the suspects. "We've got to go out to Cat Cove now and phone our supervisor, Norman Muise. We're going to get a helicopter to come down here and check to see how many more caribou you fellows killed."

Don and Christian got ready to go to Cat Cove. Before leaving, he warned the men, "If you fellows leave this cabin, we're going to charge you with escaping custody. You're under arrest, boys. Just remember that! That offense is covered by the Criminal Code, and it's a serious one. Bob Way will be left here with you, and if you do anything to him, or give him trouble in any way, you might think you're in trouble now, but you'll be in an awful scrape then, boys!"

With that, they left and travelled out to Cat Cove, where they made their phone calls. Soon they left again, heading back to camp. Before they arrived there, however, the helicopter flew over. They signalled, and the craft landed nearby. They told the pilot to proceed to the cabin and land. Half an hour later, they arrived at the camp.

In the meantime, Bob had visitors. Some of the men's friends went looking for them after they were apprehended. In the morning, they arrived at the camp and tried to give Bob a rough time. He warned them, telling them there would be trouble, so they left.

They used the helicopter to make a complete check of the area to see how much damage these fellows had done. They had an idea they could have killed more caribou there. There were injured caribou running everywhere on the country. What a mess these fellows had made! Nobody knows how many caribou perished there.

After organizing everything, they air-lifted the meat and the other things out to Hawke's Bay. They took the men who were under arrest to the police station at Port Saunders. John had to go to the hospital to have his leg X-rayed. Luckily, it wasn't broken, but it was sore for a long time!

The men appeared in court and were fined heavily, barely escaping jail sentences. Following court work, one of them passed near John as he left the room.

"Boy oh boy!" he said. "John, what an explosion! What a fright!"

He couldn't forget the explosion in the cabin when John had thrown gasoline onto the hot coals in the stove. It made quite an impression on him, and probably gave him a fright he'll always remember!

Chapter 8

The Cat Cove Investigation Continued

N ow," John said to Randy Trask, "that situation was nearly the same as the one we're in right now. The main thing I remember is that we played our cards right that night. We did all of the right things that helped us to come out on top. It's the same now. Although it may take awhile, and we might have to go through a lot of trouble, if we do the right things, we should catch these lads.

"I'm pretty sure that, unless something quite unusual has happened outside to stop them, they will be back. So all we have to do now is to hang in there. I believe we're going to succeed in the end, and keep remembering that, even if we're in here for a week or so! If we make the right moves this time, we'll have no problems. The guilty ones will be caught and punished."

They spent the rest of the night talking, listening, and watching, but nobody came in for the moose during the long night. The weather was freezing cold, and the snow became as hard as ice. These conditions were in their favour because they knew they could investigate without leaving any boot tracks.

As dawn broke on Friday, May 17, 1985, they moved out of their position. They started down the small ridge, along the brook at its base, following the snowmobile and snowshoe tracks. Almost a hundred and fifty yards ahead, they discovered another dead moose, apparently felled by the same person. Checking closer, they saw it was a cow. The only parts of the animal that had been left were the head and legs. These pieces were buried under boughs. Further investigation revealed three empty 30-30 shells. They marked and tagged the shells as Exhibit #4.

They double-checked the tracks, making sure no other people were involved. They noticed that the moose had been shot at close range. This was probably because of the deep snow and the hard travelling conditions for the moose while carrying a calf. They looked the situation over closely, and were finally able to piece together the loose ends.

The two men had come in on a snowmobile each. There were five moose yarded up at the end of the pond. They shot one moose (kill #1); the other four animals started to climb with some difficulty up the small ridge along the cutover. One man on snowshoes chased the four animals, killing another cow (Kill #2) before the other three could reach the large timber. He came back to Kill #1 and paunched the animal. Next, the poachers took their snowmobiles and went to Kill #2, and pulled the paunch out of it. They returned to Kill #1. This explains why the operation appeared to be a fast job. They cut moose #1 in two long pieces; each man hooked half to his snowmobile and headed out to Cat Cove.

The sun was rising, and the snow was as hard as flint. Randy sniffed the snow like a hound-dog when they got out on the pond. There, they saw where the three other moose had come down from the ridge.

At the scene of Kill #2, they pieced together what had happened. The three moose that had tried to escape by going over the ridge, later came back to the pond and went out toward Cat Cove, travelling in the snowmobile tracks. The signs indicated that the men were dragging their kill on top of the tracks made by the three moose that had fled toward Cat Cove.

John and Randy followed the tracks, and saw where one moose had turned right, leaving the pond on the south side. The other two moose went on out toward Cat Cove. As they walked on down the pond, John noticed a snowmobile track on the north side. Randy stayed on the main track, while John turned off to investigate this new sign.

He saw that this was the track of one of the men who had come in from Cat Cove. It kept to the north side. He observed where the man had gotten off his snowmobile and walked into the woods. He had gone to a large tree, reached in and got a gun. John stooped and examined the print of the gun-butt. The hunter had come back out, boarded his snowmobile, and gone straight over to the moose kills. Their informant had said that Ryland Gill had wrapped a rifle in a coat and put it on his snowmobile. Leaving home that evening, he had proceeded into the woods with Luke Greene. After seeing this, however, John knew two rifles were involved. He called Randy over and asked him to look at it. Randy agreed.

They went back to the bloody trail, and travelled on out toward Cat Cove. They crossed the pond and were walking across a bog at the east end when they saw where a moose had come back on the trail and gone to the south side. They noticed numerous crows in this direction, but were unable to investigate due to a lack of time. They continued their journey out along the trail.

They had gone only fifty feet when they noticed a pool of blood at the end of the bog. There were tracks where a snowmobile pulling a moose had stopped.

They also noticed that the two moose that had gone on ahead toward Cat Cove had doubled back and joined the lone moose that had branched off on the bog.

At this spot, the hunters had shot another moose; this was Kill #3. The officers carefully looked around and found three empty 30-30 shells that they marked Exhibit #5. This one had been shot at close range. It wasn't hard to understand what had happened here. These men had met up with the two moose that had probably been spooked by some activity in the town, so they doubled back, refusing to leave the trail, which took them back to the pond. Unfortunately, on the bog, they met the two men with a moose in tow. The men had opened fire, killing a large cow. The wardens were not able to determine if the other one was wounded, because they didn't have time to investigate any further; they already had enough on their hands.

As they moved down the hill at the end of the bog, the two officers saw the four quarters of the cow moose stashed away under a tree. The poachers had shot the animal on the bog, pulled it down over the hill where it was out of sight, then paunched it.

The two hunters had cut open the cow. The two calves ready to be born must have been kicking them. They took out the sac containing the calves, then separated the sac from the paunch. They dragged it away ten feet, dug a hole and threw it in. When John and Randy arrived on the scene, they checked the paunch, but there was no sac.

"What's this?" John asked Randy. "Let's check this area for calves."

He checked around with his axe, and found a hollow spot in the snow. When he struck the hard snow, the top caved in.

"Hey!" he shouted. "Come and look at this! There's something in here!"

He chopped the hole larger and put his hand inside. John could feel the sac and the shape of a calf.

"I've found it!" he said. "Come here and see!"

Randy came closer. His partner cut open the sac and inserted his hand. He caught hold of the head of a calf.

"Just watch this," he instructed. He lifted the sac up and pulled the head out. They could hardly believe their eyes!

He continued to lift it until it was completely out. The calf was about the size of a large dog. It was red, and its eyes were open. The body was fully formed, and the hooves were a dark grey. This was a sign that the calves were ready to be born.

He put it down and reached inside the sac for the second time.

"Randy," he said, "there's another one inside here. Good Lord!"

He pulled out the head. The eyes of this young calf looked at them in silence, a silence that condemned man's brutality that would butcher the innocent unborn. He stood still, lost in thought. Regaining his composure, he turned to Randy. "It's just horrible!

Imagine. They never had the chance to be born!" The old cow had survived the bitter cold and sleet of winter, only to be slaughtered just before she calved. They looked at the mess before them.

"Randy, what do you think of this?"

"I think these two men must be insane!" he answered.

"You're right! If ever there was a need to catch these fellows, it is now!"

"I guess it is."

John Christian had laid hundreds of wildlife charges—big game violations. In 1985 alone, he laid approximately fifty-five big game charges. He had also seen many gruesome things happen to wildlife, such as moose being snared and axed to death by poachers, to mention a couple. Slaughter after slaughter had taken place, but the carnage in the Cat Cove area on this morning made him weep. Sick and disgusting, it was a sight he never forgot.

John lifted the two calves and placed them back into the hole. He hung his head and prayed, "Lord, I need help from you. You own the cattle on a thousand hills, and I know you care about them. Help us to bring these people to justice. Amen."

They headed toward town, walking cautiously in the early morning sun. They had covered about a mile when they came to a high hill overlooking the west part of Cat Cove. They knew that if they went any farther, they would expose themselves to prying eyes. They checked the houses in the town, but saw no smoke rising from the chimneys.

Under cover, they walked downhill toward the town. Reaching the base of the hill, they stopped and checked again, but still couldn't see anybody moving. They continued their investigation at the base of the hill. Ahead of them was the hydro plant, with its roaring diesel. They knew they would have to stay clear of this place, because Luke Greene's father was the chief operator there.

John had caught Simon Greene twice before, and each time he received heavy fines. He also had him in court in 1984, but his lawyer got him off on a plea bargain. His younger son took the rap for him.

Between the base of the hill and the hydro plant, there was a wooded area. This was the area that interested John. He wanted to have a close look around the woods.

Nearing the area, John spotted the tracks of local dogs, a sure indication that something edible was hidden in the woods. Their search revealed a front quarter of moose and part of a hind quarter hidden there. The meat was fresh, and matched the quarters of moose #1. They left it where it was.

They sat down for a few minutes, trying to piece everything together. So many questions that seemed to have no answers were going through their minds: *What reason did they have for not coming back to get the meat? Why weren't they in yet to get the ten quarters left in the woods?*

They couldn't think of any answers to their questions.

Usually, Ryland Gill would risk almost anything, but right now it didn't appear to be that way. Maybe he was away, perhaps sealing. But even if this were the case, he would still be home at night. They knew something was wrong. Maybe he'll come back tonight, they thought.

With this in mind, they decided to head back to their base camp, walking with ease over the hill. It didn't matter now if they were noticed. If someone saw them at a distance, they would think they were just going into the woods to get firewood, or for some other purpose. They took their time.

They had asked John Ennis to come back any time after 9:00 a.m., and they could depend on him, unless he had an emergency. They needed more search warrants made out. They said many unfavourable things about the new Charter of Rights. It was because of the Charter's rules that they needed the search warrants, and obtain them they would; there was no arguing that point. Sitting in their tent, they made their plans, deciding what to do next.

They knew that two quarters of the moose had already gone into town. If they searched and found meat in Ryland and Luke's homes, it still would not be enough to tie them in with the current mess. They realized the importance of catching them in the very act. It appeared they would have to stay for at least another night. If they didn't catch them at the kill site, they decided to search for the rifles. With any luck at all, they might be able to seize them. They knew it would be next to impossible to obtain a statement from anyone in the town. Ryland's father was the main businessman in Cat Cove, and Luke's father the chief operator of the hydro plant. But there was still an angle John could use to get the information he needed.

He knew the people of Cat Cove well. Only a few people there were involved in poaching, and most of it was done when they started drinking. He knew that if he put a couple of these calves on display in the centre of the town, someone would inform on the boys. That is, if they didn't catch them in the act themselves!

He hadn't heard the forecast, but he knew the good weather they were enjoying wasn't going to last much longer. Once the rain started, all the brooks would overflow their banks. The rain was long overdue.

After a meal, they went back to the pond and waited for the helicopter. They waited until 1:30 p.m., when John Ennis finally arrived. He reported he had had an emergency on the south coast, and was unable to get back earlier. He also informed the officers that Clarence Maloney had sent men into Doctor's hills to take out the snowmobiles they had seized the day before.

To Ennis, one of them said, "We have to go to Roddickton for more search warrants."

"Boys," he said, "you're going to have to get your work done fast, because there's a big rain on the way, and it's supposed to hit the Northern Peninsula this afternoon."

"Okay," Christian said. "We'll hurry things up."

Boarding the helicopter, they told the pilot to take them directly to Roddickton.

"Okay," Ennis replied as they lifted off.

They went to Roddickton, where they had search warrants drawn up. They noticed the bad weather moving in fast and lost no time flying back to their outpost area.

John Ennis let them out in the rain, and left without cutting the engine speed. The officers asked him to brief Clarence Maloney the moment he arrived at Pasadena. They went to their tent and laid out plans, knowing that they would have to change their outpost, and set one up near Moose # 3, closer to the town.

They packed a lunch-bag, and took the items they would need: plastic, flashlights and writing material. If nobody came in to get the moose overnight, they would go to Cat Cove in the morning and carry out their search. They agreed that the main items to seize were 30-30 rifles. There were two involved in this case, and they knew that their best chance at making any charges stick would be a positive ballistics test involving the shells they had found. They were in possession of three moose heads—and there were head shots—so they were certain there were slugs in the meat. Now all they needed were the rifles that they were sure could be found on someone's property.

They put on their snowshoes and started toward Moose #3, but had a difficult time. The rain had turned the snow to slush, making it almost impossible to walk on snowshoes. They had to be careful when stopping near the trees, for fear of sinking beside them. This made the task of pulling their legs out of the holes unusually difficult. It took them more than an hour in these conditions to travel one mile. They were also slowed down because they had to keep off the trail to avoid being spotted.

Arriving at the area they had selected, they decided to set up the outpost on the opposite side of the trail near the moose. They were within two miles of the town. They blocked the trail with felled trees, and positioned themselves in such a way that, if anyone arrived and stopped, they could overhear and record any comments or conversation they made.

They quickly went to work, camouflaging their positions. They had to ensure that the poachers had come for meat and not for firewood, knowing they would use any excuse if brought to court. Darkness soon fell. The drizzle and the fog made conditions miserable. Randy thought he heard snowmobiles twice, but each time proved to be a false alarm. They passed

a couple of hours talking about the wholesale slaughter
of moose.

John told Randy about a case he had been
involved in near Croque a week or two earlier.

A small fishing community south of St. Anthony,
Croque is located at Epine Cadoret Inlet on the
northeast shore of the bay known as Croque Harbour.

At that time, Wildlife caught three men who were
poaching. They had killed three moose, one of which
was carrying twin calves. The men were later convicted
in court and got large fines. One of them received, in
addition to a fine, ninety days in jail. Each of them was
prohibited from holding a big game licence for five
years.

A few days before, John had chased two men on
the back of Doctor's Hills. They had killed two caribou.
One of the animals had a large fawn ready to be born.

It had been a year of one slaughter after another.

Chapter 9

Rendezvous at Cat Cove

It was wet, cold, and late in the night when John and Randy decided to make another move. By now, anyone coming in would encounter great difficulty. The conditions for moose hunting or transporting moose were excellent earlier in the evening, but nobody had come, and it was unlikely anyone would show up under these conditions. Figuring something was wrong, they decided to move into town, remain under cover, and conduct their search in the morning.

They set out from the outpost and started travelling toward Cat Cove, walking cautiously into the driving rain. John informed Randy that he knew a man in town who would be more than willing to take them into his house and hide them until morning. He wasn't an informant, but he disliked poaching and wanted to see it stopped—or at least slowed down. John felt sure that when he told him about this senseless slaughter, he would take them in.

They walked out to the hilltop and looked down over the town. They could hear the roaring sound of the diesel engine.

"I wonder what went wrong, Randy?" John said. "I mean, why didn't they come back for all of the meat?"

"I don't have any idea," he said.

"Our main problem now is the dogs. If they start barking and come at us, they might alert someone," he said.

They also knew they would encounter problems getting past the hydro plant. The plant had a steel fence around it, and there was a large, bright street light at its entrance. The road they had to follow went almost directly under the light-pole. The area was dry, but they couldn't walk down the street without beeing seen. The route they would have to take, around the outskirts of town and through back yards, meant crossing the brook and through flooded areas.

"Well, Randy," John said, "do you have a suggestion?"

Randy continued to study the area slowly. "It looks like a problem all right," he said.

They both looked the area over again.

"You'll have to make the decision," Randy said. "It's all up to you now!"

"Well, it's like this, Randy," John said as he peered at him through the driving rain. He could see water streaming down Randy's face. "If the Norwegians in Oslo could get through all of the guards and blow up a heavy water plant, then we should certainly be able to pull this one off without getting caught!"

Randy grinned. He took off his glasses and wiped the water from them. John knew he had plenty of courage, and he knew Randy would back him up in anything he did.

"This job isn't for the faint-hearted, Randy," he said. "You know that. They're going to get caught and they're going to pay!"

They moved farther downhill. They checked the moose quarters they had stashed away earlier that morning. They hadn't been moved. They walked on. Drawing near the plant, they noticed that all of the snow near the plant was gone.

"Randy," John whispered, "we'll take off our snowshoes and make a run for it."

They crept along, getting closer to the plant. About a hundred feet from the light-pole, there was a brightly-lit house, a sure sign that the occupants were still up. They continued to move cautiously. They were now clearly visible to anyone who might be looking their way.

Suddenly, John noticed three snowmobiles near the entrance to the plant. One of the machines had a sleigh hitched to it, as well as a box on the sleigh.

"Look at that!" he said. "That's part of the gang!"

They surveyed where they had to go in order to avoid being seen. The only way to remain hidden was to go behind the houses in the dark. To do this, however, they would first have to go within one foot of the light-pole before hitting the swollen brook.

"We have no choice," John said. "It has to be done."

They took off their snowshoes. " Let's go!" he said. Both of them raced to the pole. John sank down in the snow and had to put on his snowshoes to get moving again. With luck on their side, they escaped detection.

"Boy, that was a close one!" Randy said.

"Just look here," John said. They were facing the brook. In order to go any farther, they would have to wade across. "Let's go!" he said.

They stepped into the brook. John was wearing ranger-issue winter boots, with felts and a drawstring at the top. Randy was wearing felted winter boots, too, and they were both wearing snowshoes. They were floundering around in the water, with slush up to their knees, not knowing when they would sink. They were also fearful that the local dogs could come at them at any moment, and they ran the risk of being seen by the wrong people.

They passed a house where the occupants' son had been caught in 1984 with moose killed illegally; he had received a $1,500.00 fine in court.

The officers knew that even if there was the slightest suspicion that they were in town, their chances of catching anyone would be slim. This far along in their investigations, it was essential to remain hidden and not take any unnecessary risks.

They managed to cross the brook and arrived at a house belonging to a man by the name of Ralph Randell. There was a light burning in the living room.

"It looks like he's still up," John whispered.

"Good," said Randy.

"You're going to have to hide here while I go check things out."

"Good enough. I'll do that."

"Now, be sure to stay out of sight."

"All right."

John hid Randy in an old shed nearby.

"Well, here goes," he said. He looked closely at the surrounding buildings, then at the road. Seeing nobody, he moved swiftly to the door and knocked. Through the glass in the door, John could see someone coming downstairs. The door opened, and Ralph's twelve-year-old son, Christopher, looked at him, wide-eyed. The boy recognized him; he had been at the same home about a month before and had had a lunch with Ralph.

Evidence of blood on the hills. Here, Wildlife Officer Earl Pilgrim (John Christian) holds up an unborn calf, the results of the carnage of poachers on the Great Northern Peninsula. Scenes like this inspired Earl Pilgrim to wipe out illegal big game hunting.

Wildlife cabin on Cloud River.

A bull moose disturbed from its winter yard.

Gunner's Cove moose rescue. This cow moose fell through the ice. Wildlife Officer Earl Pilgrim (John Christian) and R.C.M.P. Staff Sergeant Jerry Locke organized a rescue using sleds and ropes. Earl held her head as others placed a rope around the animal and pulled her out. Frightened, the animal turned away from the men and ran into the hole again. The second rescue attempt was successful when the rescuers stood blocking the hole.

Gunner's Cove moose rescue. Here, Wildlife Officer Earl Pilgrim (John Christian) successfully massages the chest of the unconscious cow moose suffering from hypothermia. The animal revived and was driven into the heavy woods nearby. In the spring she had her two calves.

The Pollard case. Calvin Pollard was responsible for killing this cow without knowing she was pregnant. To make a point about poaching, Wildlife Officer Earl Pilgrim (John Christian) tried to shame and shock him into changing his behaviour by having him view this scene, a fetus laid across its mother's head.

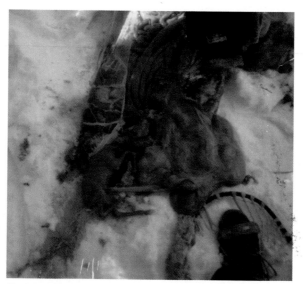

The Pollard case. A moose fetus lies in the snow, still attached to the umbilical cord and paunch.

A poacher's trail tucked away in the heavy woods.

An illegal summer kill.

Moose killed by a head shot. For ballistics tests, bullets had to be cut out of the skull.

Calves never born. Evidence secured at Wildlife's storage shed at Pasadena, Newfoundland.

Confiscated quarters of moose and impounded snowmobiles at the Wildlife storage shed at Pasadena, Newfoundland.

The Ryland Gill case. Twin calves never born. Wildlife Officer Earl Pilgrim (John Christian) placed these two calves on public display in Cat Cove to shock the townspeople and encourage them to report any poaching they witnessed.

Wildlife Officer Earl Pilgrim (John Christian) with a caribou calf during a survey on the Grey Islands.

Wildlife Officer Earl Pilgrim (John Christian). The mother of these calves was struck by a vehicle. Officer Pilgrim decided to give the animal a chance to have her calves. Injured, the cow moose crawled into the nearby woods and had these calves the same night. When Earl visited them, the calves followed him out of the woods, but he doubled back to their mother and ducked out of sight. The cow nursed her calves long enough to survive on their own.

"Is your father home?" he whispered.

"Yes."

He held up his hand and motioned for him to remain quiet. He turned and went upstairs, tiptoeing softly. John stepped inside, and was glad to be there in the warmth. As he closed the door behind him, he heard someone stirring upstairs. Ralph came into view, and ran downstairs with a rhythmic speed.

"John!" he exclaimed. "Where in the world did you come from?"

Chapter 10

The Hydro Plant:
Friendly Watchers

John stood in the porch while the rain poured outside. He was wet, cold and hungry, looking like something the sea had tossed upon the beach in a storm.

Ralph motioned to him to get away from the window.

"I have a buddy with me," John said. "He's hidden outside."

"Get him in here right away!"

John made a motion toward the door.

"No, stop!" Ralph said. "Not that way! Go and get him to come into the basement through the back door."

"Good!" John said.

They went down to the basement where Ralph opened the door to let John out. He went to the shed and called in a low voice to Randy. "Come on!" he said.

As they were walking toward the basement, Ralph opened the door to let the two officers in, and then closed the door to the elements. There was enough light in the basement for them to see each other fairly well. John introduced Randy to Ralph.

Ralph motioned for his son to go upstairs, and he obeyed.

"Boys, where did you come from?" Ralph asked.

"We were on a stakeout by a moose kill, trying to catch the men who killed them," John answered.

"You know, John, I kind of suspected that some fellas here killed a moose. Everybody else around here knows it, too."

"Ralph," John continued, "they shot three old cows. The calves are as big as dogs!"

Ralph could hardly believe what he was hearing. "It's getting worse all the time, John."

"I wonder why they didn't come back for the meat," John said. "You know, we've been in there hiding for a day and half, but nobody has shown up yet. There must be something wrong somewhere. Do you have any idea what it could be?"

"I know that after Ryland Gill and Luke Greene shot the moose, they came out," Ralph said. "When Ryland went home, he discovered that his young son had fallen down and broken his arm. He had to leave by boat right away for the hospital at Roddickton. After he got to Roddickton, he had to go to St. Anthony for more specialized treatment. With Ryland gone, the others didn't have the nerve to go in after the meat. Then someone said they heard a helicopter there yesterday."

"Well," John said, "I guess that ends that."

"No, it doesn't end it!" Ralph replied.

"Why not?"

"Did you come down along the power house?"

"Yes, we did."

Ralph continued, "Well, there are supposed to be three snowmobiles up there. One has a sleigh, with a box on it, in tow."

"You're right. We saw them there."

"Well now, then that's the three lads who were about to go for a load of meat."

"Who are they?"

"Your old buddies," Ralph replied, grinning from ear to ear, "Mike Lane, Will Hiscock and the honourable Sy Greene," ending with a note of sarcasm.

John knew very well who they were. He had caught Michael Lane and Will Hiscock in 1984. They were convicted, each of them receiving a $1000.00 fine. Both of them also lost their snowmobiles and were prohibited from holding a big game licence for five years.

"I've got to get back to the power house and see what's going on," he said.

"It's a bad night to have to go out," Ralph said kindly, "but these men deserve to get caught."

"I guess they do!" John said. "Randy, you can stay here if you want to. I am going on a look-see patrol. If I need any help, I'll be back for you."

"Okay," Randy said. "Do you think you can make it alone all right?"

"Sure I can," he said, "and what's more, one man won't be as noticeable as two would be."

It was past midnight, and the rain was pelting down. John put on his snowshoes and stepped outside.

"Lot's of luck," Ralph and Randy called.

"Thanks. I'm going to need it."

They closed the door behind him, and he walked back the same way he and Randy had come. John moved a little faster and closely watched the houses. The light on the pole near the power house could be seen through the beating rain. It shone brightly in his eyes, and he had to shade them as he got closer.

Finally, he reached the area near the house that was closest to the plant. He would still have to pass under the bright light. It was the only route he could follow, unless he walked on the road. The dwelling was still brightly lit. He moved closer to look at the plant. The three snowmobiles were still there, one with a box on a sleigh. John decided to get as close as possible.

He looked again at the house, then moved toward the light-pole. While in the Canadian Army, he had learned never to move fast at night when there was light around. Movement was a deadly enemy. He moved carefully, ready to stop at the first sign of recognition. Nobody came to the house windows; it seemed that he had escaped detection. He found himself directly under the street light, hugging the light-pole.

He quickly surveyed the hydro yard and spotted half a dozen oil barrels in the centre. A bunch of wire was coiled near them. He decided this would be his hiding place, about twenty feet from the snowmobiles. As he moved toward the barrels, he could see one of the men through the windows in front of him.

He reached the barrels and hid securely among them. Nervously, he looked back at the house; nobody was watching. He peered over the barrels at the power plant. In the office, someone was sitting at the table.

Suddenly, the door burst open, and out came Michael Lane. He stood on the bridge, talking to someone still in the plant. Next, Will Hiscock walked out. The two men stepped from the bridge while continuing to talk with Sy Greene, who was standing in the doorway. Christian couldn't hear their conversation because of the roar of the diesel, but by the motions they were making, he suspected they were saying their "good nights."

It was raining torrents now. The men started their snowmobiles and turned around in the yard. At one point, their lights shone directly on John, tucked down among the barrels. He hugged the messy ground, covered in soot and black oil. The three men left, going down the road and out of sight toward their homes.

John turned toward the plant and watched as Sy Greene went to the main office at the far side of the plant. John had to shift his position to follow Sy's movements, and in doing so, put himself in full view of the brightly-lit plant. Sy opened a door close to John, and began to start a diesel engine. Sy walked near the engine and put his ear to the sound. Then he watched the gauges and checked the machine again. He grabbed a chair and set it in the doorway. He sat down, seeming to gaze straight toward John's location. John was amazed that Sy didn't see him in the yard, where he was still as a mouse.

After awhile, Sy Greene got up and put on his coat. He rechecked the gauges and shut down the engine. Closing the door, he walked to the other side of the plant to the office, where he checked a few meters. He came out, shutting the door behind him, walked to his snowmobile and unhooked the sleigh. By now, John had shifted into his initial position, not exposed in the brightest area.

Sy started his snowmobile, and though his lights were shining directly on the officer, he left the yard, leaving John alone. When the machine was out of sight, he stood up, walked to the sleigh and checked the box on it, but found it empty. He went to the plant, opened the door, and looked inside, but still saw nothing. He checked the back of the building. Still nothing.

John walked back to the oil barrels and decided to wait there. He figured the men would go home, have a lunch, then go in for the meat. Suddenly, he discovered he was being watched! This took him completely by surprise.

A man and a woman in the nearby house were watching him through the windows! They were moving from window to window, and then going to their bridge to get a better look. He thought quickly. There was nowhere else for him to go. He and Randy Trask were the only law officers in the town at the moment. There were no Mounties to be called, and here he was—pinned down, and really in trouble! But he had to make a move. He made up his mind to walk out of the yard, in full view of the house. It was the only thing he could do.

He stood, pulled his hood over his face, tucked his snowshoes under his arm, and walked toward the house. He turned the fence corner and walked briskly down the road. Out of the corner of his eye, he could see that the watchers were still moving from one window to another.

John trudged back toward Ralph Randell's house. To his knowledge, the only people besides Ralph who knew he was in Cat Cove were the young man and woman who saw him at the power plant. When he reached Ralph's house, it was 2:00 a.m. and he was wet and hungry. Ralph wanted to know all of the details about what had happened since he had left the house.

He described his activities over the last few days, step by step. He hung up his wet clothes in the furnace room and went upstairs, where all were welcomed by Ralph's wife Lillian. Randy and John sat with Ralph and ate a steaming hot meal. Sitting with Ralph at the table was an entertaining time in itself. Mrs. Randell had prepared a meal of baked chicken, and John was sure it was the most delicious meal he had ever eaten!

After they ate, Ralph said he wanted to know about a poaching incident that had taken place at Port Au Choix a couple of months earlier.

"Okay, Ralph," John said. " Now, let me see. Where do I begin? Oh, yes."

John proceeded to tell Ralph about the capture of four poachers in one day.

Chapter 11

The Port au Choix Incident: Four Tired Poachers

On February 27, 1985, while alone on a wildlife patrol in the Port Saunders area, not far from Port au Choix, John Christian left his pickup around 1:30 in the afternoon and proceeded on snowmobile toward Big East River.

About a kilometre in from the truck, he crossed a small pond. At the end of the pond, he saw snowmobile tracks leading from a cabin. He noticed that they went in toward Big East River.

It was not a good evening, with blowing snow and whiteout conditions. John followed the tracks with difficulty for ten kilometres to a cabin owned by James Breene of Port au Choix. He discovered that the fire was still burning in the stove. After examining the tracks and comparing them, he figured the people involved had waited in the cabin for one or two hours before leaving again.

The tracks led from the cabin up a hill known locally as Wiggies Hill. There were four machines in all. John noted that at least two snowmobiles were towing sleighs behind them. He knew that the people on the machines certainly weren't on a joyride, considering the present weather conditions.

He followed their tracks for about seven kilometres to Kelly's cabin. The weather was starting to thicken with snow and drizzle. He followed them out on the open country for approximately four kilometres.

The tracks then turned right, and went down on a transmission line. This was puzzling. He thought he had been following caribou hunters, but this was decidedly different. *Maybe they aren't caribou hunters after all,* he thought.

He continued down the transmission line two kilometres to Wiggies Gulch, to a brook, still following the tracks. He went out the brook another two kilometres, then turned left to a bog. There he saw four snowmobiles—two twelve-horsepower Elan Ski-doos, one Bravo Yamaha, and one new Bravo Transporter Yamaha, along with four sleighs. Two had racks built on them for hauling meat.

He stopped near the machines, noticing snowshoe tracks leading into the woods from each one. He also saw that each of the men had removed his coat and laid it on his snowmobile. This was easily understood. By now the weather had turned really warm, and there was a fine, misty rain falling.

He thought for a moment, wondering how he was going to catch these men. Until then, he had nothing to go on, only a suspicion that poaching was taking place there.

He recorded the plate numbers of the snowmobiles, and decided to try to trick the men into returning to their machines. He put on his snowshoes and walked into the woods on top of their snowmobile tracks, and then waited for a few minutes. He then came back quickly over his own tracks. The suspects were just about to start their machines.

One of them saw him, and the other three ran. He recognized two of them. One was James Breene of Port au Choix, but he couldn't call the other men by name. The incident happened too fast for him to get a quick look at the third man. He was unable to run into the woods after them, because he would have had to leave his snowmobile unattended, and he knew that one of them could return while he was away and damage it. He was about twenty miles in the country at the time and could not risk that. When he considered what had happened, he knew there was something wrong.

He went to the four snowmobiles and investigated each one. He noticed the men had been cutting a trail down a hill leading to a small brook. This was where they had come from when John saw them near their snowmobiles.

He thought, *What am I going to do now?* He needed some solid evidence to act on.

He took the Bravo Transporter and ran it into the woods, where he hid it. He decided to take a gamble and look around. He walked into the woods over their snowshoe tracks. A couple of hundred yards ahead, he found an area where moose were yarding up. He knew then what was going on: they were after moose!

He continued, still following the men's tracks. They went around in a circle, and then started walking toward the snowmobiles. He looked around, and caught sight of what he was looking for—four quarters of moose hanging up in the trees. Walking on for another thirty or so feet, he saw four more quarters hanging up. Now he had all the evidence he needed.

He followed the tracks in a straight line to the snowmobiles. When he got there, he checked the clothing they had left on their machines. In the pocket of one parka, he found a sealing licence # 118550, issued in 1984. The name on the licence was Don Walsh of Port au Choix, Newfoundland. A crest on another coat said, "Security and Safety Department, San Antonio, Texas."

Christian went back into the woods for a further look, and decided that two men had gone out the brook, and two had turned in the brook. At that time, it appeared to be a well-planned operation.

He returned to the bog, put three snowmobiles out of operation, and left one for their safety. He left their clothing and lunches. He now realized that if he were planning to catch the four men, he would need help. He quickly left the area and went back to his truck.

He drove quickly to the Department of Highways depot, and called the Port Saunders Detachment of the R.C.M.P. When they heard his story, they agreed to assist him. Next he called Clarence Maloney at Pasadena, who agreed to send Wildlife Officers Sam Thornhill and Henry Humber to help.

When the R.C.M.P. officers arrived, they left their vehicles, and John led them back into the country. Arriving there, they noticed that the four men hadn't returned to their snowmobiles. They wasted no time in that area, because they knew they would really have to move fast to catch the poachers, now on foot. They headed out toward the bog area between the open country and the coast. On the way out, they met Sam Thornhill and Henry Humber, who were on their way in to meet them.

First they went to James Breene's cabin. Other than themselves and another visitor, John Riggs, nobody had been there since Breene and his company left early in the afternoon. They decided to investigate the West Lake area.

As they took the trail going there, they discovered the snowshoe tracks of four men. These tracks came from the woods in the direction where John had earlier seized the four snowmobiles. The party of lawmen got on the tracks, and started to follow them.

They seemed to be following a Ski-doo track made by John Riggs, heading for the Hawke's Bay area. The officers followed for a kilometre or so, before they saw the tracks leaving the trail and going into the woods. Henry and Constable White put on their snowshoes and walked in pursuit. Constable Ricketts and John Christian went around the woods area to check out the other side.

By the tracks in the woods, they soon discovered that the men had come out on the west side, and were heading in the direction of Hawke's Bay. They followed the tracks for another two kilometres. The officers almost caught up to them in the centre of a large bog, but they dashed into the woods and were now out of sight. John lashed on his snowshoes and chased them. He followed them for a kilometre through the woods, only to discover that they had gone into the Big East Gorge and were walking out on the river.

John came back to the Ski-doo to regroup and make more plans. He sent Henry and Sam out to patrol near the highway, in case the men exited there. John and the two R.C.M.P. officers went back on the Big East River and crossed it. They decided to come west on the new transmission line and cut the men off. They knew they were definitely heading toward the highway near Hawke's Bay. They travelled the whole length of the transmission line, all the way to Big East River, but saw no sign of snowshoe tracks. They went on the river for two kilometres and discovered that the four men had left it, and were headed toward the transmission line. They patrolled east on the line but saw nothing. They were not disappointed, however. They knew the men were cornered in this section of the woods.

By a stroke of luck, John spotted their tracks where they were about to cross the transmission line. He fastened his snowshoes and went after them. The woods area was thick, and the snow was extremely deep, so it wasn't easy trying to walk fast enough to catch them.

It was now 1:00 a.m. The weather was fairly mild, but was on the verge of turning severely cold.

John followed the men for two or three hundred yards. Suddenly, he saw someone ahead of him. He called out, but nobody answered. He hurried on as fast as he was able to travel. He could smell the stench of the camp, along with the usual smells people have on their clothing when they're spending most of their time around cabins and Ski-doos. John knew that he was closing in on the suspects.

He stepped up his pace, but suddenly came to a standstill; he nearly stepped on a man lying face-down in the snow. Though his flashlight was dull, when he shone it on the man's face, he recognized him right away. It was Don Walsh from Port au Choix, one of the men who had run away when he saw John near the snowmobiles back in the country earlier in the day.

"Don, you're under arrest!" John said. He cautioned him, and asked him the names of the other men who were with him.

He refused to co-operate. He was fatigued, and it looked like he would collapse at any time. John marched him to the right-of-way—near the transmission line—and handed him over to the R.C.M.P. officers there.

He left and went back into the woods again, where he soon got on the trail of the other three men. He followed them for two or three hundred yards. John saw where one of them had separated from the others and decided to follow the single track. Soon, he came upon this fellow, sitting in the snow near a tree, too exhausted to get up.

"Sir, you're caught!" John said. "What's your name?"

"Enos Penney."

After he was cautioned, John asked, "What are you doing here?"

"I'm making the game wardens do some work!"

"Yes," John said, "and I guess you could say I'm making you fellows work, too!"

He said nothing to this statement. John asked him for the names of the other two fellows, but he wouldn't reveal them.

He said his foot had come out of his snowshoe sling, and he was unable to go any farther. He didn't have any strength left to move.

"Where's Don?" he suddenly asked. "Have you got him?"

"Yes," John answered, "we've arrested Don. And now you're under arrest!"

He asked the officer for a drink.

John told him he didn't have anything to offer. He advised the man to follow his tracks back. "You'll come to the transmission line," he said, "and the R.C.M.P. officers will be waiting there for you."

"Yes," he said, resigned to his fate. "I'll do that and be glad to."

John left him and picked up the tracks of the two remaining men. He had two down, and two to go! So far, so good! He followed the two men's tracks at a fast pace now.

Suddenly, to his complete surprise, there they were, right in front of him! He hadn't expected to catch up with them so quickly.

By this time, his flashlight was too dull to enable him to see anything. The men dashed for the woods. John yelled for them to stop, but they ignored the command. It would be almost impossible to catch them now because of the darkness and the heavy woods he had to go through. John would have to come up with another plan if he were going to catch them.

He went back to the snowmobiles, and departed for his truck that was on the highway. The two Mounties followed with the two prisoners on their machines.

Arriving at his truck, John loaded his snowmoblie aboard the vehicle. Constables White and Ricketts arrived with the two prisoners. By now, it was severely cold, and the wind was blowing northwest. Their clothing was frozen so solid that they could hardly bend their legs and arms. They loaded the police snowmobiles aboard their truck and put Don Walsh and Enos Penney aboard John's truck. Constable Ricketts and John walked to the window and asked who the other two men were.

The prisoners said they didn't know.

John and Ricketts moved to the rear of the truck, far enough so the prisoners wouldn't hear them. "Ricketts," he said, "I'm going to see if I can bluff them into telling us the names of the other two men. Come on!"

They went back to the truck window. The weather had now turned fierce, and the wind was northwest, blowing icicles and snow. It was unusually cold. John tapped on the side window, and one of the men rolled it down.

"Now listen, boys," he said sternly. "Do you know what kind of night this is? I mean—do you really know what the conditions are like? It's blizzard conditions now."

They said nothing.

"There's one thing I want to make clear to the two of you," he continued. "If anything happens to either of the two men you left in the woods, the responsibility will be wholly and solely on you fellows!"

Enos didn't like what he was saying. "Now, you listen here!" he said. "This isn't our problem, and how can you blame anything on us?"

"Well, it's like this," John said, "you won't tell us their names."

"What good will that do," Don said, "if we tell you their names?"

"Well," John answered, "maybe if they heard me calling their names, they might say to themselves, 'They know who we are, so we might as well go out. We're caught anyway.'"

"I see what you mean, John," Enos said. He stopped for a moment, then continued. "Okay," he said. "Call out to Bill and James."

Bill? he thought. "I've never heard of him before. Bill who?"

"Never mind who!" Enos said. "Just ask for Bill and James."

"Okay," John said with a grin.

The two prisoners realized he had conned them into revealing the others' names.

99

They walked to the back of the truck. "We've got you, James Breene. And you, Bill!" they said. But Bill who? They would have to find out.

They got aboard John's truck, leaving the two prisoners with the Mounties, who proceeded to the police station at Port Saunders. John then raced toward the Hawke's Bay area, where he suspected the two men would come out onto the highway. Driving along in the storm, he neared the area, where he saw two sets of snowshoe tracks coming onto the road from the transmission line. He followed them for a couple hundred feet.

There they were!—the two men he had been looking for, the two who had given him so much trouble! They were hitchhiking, looking for a ride home.

John stopped when he got near them. They stared with wide eyes at the Wildlife sign on the truck door. John was sure they could hardly believe they were seeing right! They certainly hadn't expected to see *him* at that moment. *This man was everywhere!*

"Get aboard, boys!" he said. "You're caught!"

"We might as well," James said. "We're caught anyway. There's no way we can escape now."

"You have to be caught, men," John said. "You're breaking the law."

"We had a hard bout of it today," one of them said.

John read them their rights and cautioned them. He wrote down their names and dates of birth, and asked them which snowmobiles they owned. James said he owned the new Bravo Transporter. He and his buddy commented on the situation they were in, saying what fools they had been to do what they had done. They asked John what the magistrate was like for passing sentence on amateurs. They insisted that, had they known what they knew now, they wouldn't have left their machines. They were in poor condition, tired and exhausted from going through the woods for hours. John drove them to their homes in Port au Choix. It was a long hard night for all of them.

The four men appeared in court at Port au Choix. Their cases started at nine in the morning and finished at five in the afternoon. They had a lawyer represent them. The judge convicted the quartet of men, gave them a $2000.00 fine each, and prohibited them from holding a big game licence for five years.

Chapter 12

The Twin Calves

After John Christian finished relating this story to Ralph Randell, they decided it was time for bed, to catch a few hours of rest. Before retiring for the night, however, Randy Trask and John had a meeting in the privacy of John's bedroom. They decided to search two homes in the morning. They agreed that Randy would search Simon Greene's. John described for him where Simon's secret deep-freeze was hidden. They also agreed that they were looking for 30-30 rifles. If they found moose meat in refrigerators, it would only be a possessions charge. Without a statement, they would not be able to tie anyone in with the kills. But the rifles could be matched with the slugs and shells.

John knew exactly what he was after at Ryland Gill's. He was expecting to find a 30-30 rifle that would match the shells at the three kill sites, and a shotgun that would match the shot shells he had taken at the moose kill near Cat Cove on February 7, 1985.

Randy and John also decided to get help to go in and haul out the moose in the morning.

They got up at six. It had stopped raining, but it was still foggy. They ate breakfast, and at 7:30 a.m. they left Ralph's home and went to search the two houses as planned.

Randy went to Simon Greene's house.

He checked Sy's two deep-freezes, but did not find anything. While searching, though, he found one 30-30 rifle. He was told it belonged to Luke Greene, Simon's son. Simon was visibly shaken over having his house searched and the rifle seized.

John went to Ryland Gill's house.

He expected to learn that Ryland was not at home. He knocked a couple of times, and a young lady in her dressing gown came to the door. It was obvious she had been in bed. She was working at the fish plant, and was living in the basement apartment of Ryland's house. She opened the door slowly.

"Is Ryland in?" John asked.

"No, he isn't here," she said in a shaky voice. "He went to Roddickton."

"I have a search warrant here, Ma'am," John said. Through the open door, he noticed a gun rack in the porch.

"You can't search the house, sir, because Ryland isn't at home," she said.

"I have a search warrant drawn up and signed by the Justice of the Peace to search this home," he said. "And whether or not Ryland is home, I have to search."

"Okay."

He stepped into the porch. "Who owns these guns?" he asked.

"Ryland does, sir."

There were two shotguns there: one was a pump-action twelve-gauge. It was polished and shining, with not a scratch on it anywhere. At the bottom of the rack, there was another. It, too, was clean, but judging from the scars on the stock and barrel, it had received plenty of use on a snowmobile. Also, the foresight, one of the first parts of a gun to be damaged from being carried on a snowmobile in winter, had been repaired.

John continued to do a complete and thorough search of the house. He found nothing that was useful in the investigation. He opened the deep-freeze, but it was empty. He later learned that the 30-30 rifle he was looking for was hidden on the floor under the deep-freeze.

On his way out of the house, he seized the single-shot shotgun from the gun-rack. "You could be the one," he said as he picked up the weapon. "I need you."

John asked the woman to tell Ryland to contact him as soon as he arrived home. He then left and returned to Ralph Randell's house.

By now, there was much movement in the town. A number of people were on the go, because they were curious to know what was happening, or what was about to happen. The news that John Christian was in town had evidently spread.

At Ralph's house, he discovered that Randy had found the rifle he was looking for, which was actually their sole piece of evidence so far. Their next step was to use the psychological approach of bringing the moose out of the country and putting the unborn calves on display. John hoped that someone, seeing the results of the slaughter, would volunteer information or provide them with a statement.

He called Clarence Maloney at Pasadena, gave him all of the details they had, and advised him they would not be needing the helicopter because the weather was too bad. They would have to use a longliner to get out of Cat Cove. He gave his permission to hire one.

The townspeople were beginning to gather near Ralph's house, so John went out to meet with them and told them what was going on, again hoping to elicit information from someone in the community. The people confirmed that the men they were looking for were Ryland Gill and Luke Greene, but nobody was willing to give them a statement about anything they had heard or seen. Nearly everyone on hand volunteered to go into the country with the officers to help bring out the moose. Randy and John borrowed two snowmobiles, and with a dozen men set off for the country.

As they travelled, John showed them step by step how Randy and he had investigated and reconstructed the poachers' moves. The people were intrigued to find out how they operated. John knew this would have a strong impact on them, especially concerning any future poaching—which he doubted they would do. He knew that by the time this incident was told and retold a couple of more times, it would be quite the tale.

They had no problem hauling out everything in one trip. With so many helpers, they arrived at the harbour shortly before noon. They took the calves and put them in full view of the town. Before long, they noticed women and girls crying. The men were angry, saying that whoever did the poaching had to be caught and stopped.

Shortly after, John was informed that two young women were willing to provide them with a statement. They said they had seen two men going in the country with a rifle around six on Wednesday evening.

John and Randy went to their home and talked with them. John could tell they were scared to identify the men as Ryland and Luke, but their statement was nevertheless worthwhile. At least it was known in Cat Cove that they had obtained a statement from two people. They felt sure this would provide them with something to work on.

They decided not to press their luck too far by going to see Luke or Simon Greene. They had started things moving now, but they had to go slowly. In order to get enough evidence to charge Ryland and Luke, they would have to play their cards correctly.

They went back to Ralph's home for lunch. They contacted Joseph Hynes, who owned a longliner, and arranged for him to bring them to Englee, forty miles north of Cat Cove.

They later learned that Michael Lane had gone to Skipper Joseph Hynes's house on the evening of May seventeenth. Plans were laid by the men to go into the country and haul out the moose the next day. They were going to give Joe a quarter of moose if he went in with them. But his wife said to him, "Joe, I've got a funny feeling about this whole mess. You're not going in there with that crowd! I've got a feeling that this time somebody is going to get caught." Joe didn't go.

As the officers were heading to Englee aboard Joe's longliner, John asked him about this incident.

Joe looked at him and grinned. "John," he said, "just suppose I had gone in there. I sure would be in one awful mess today!"

"John," he continued, "how did you ever get involved in this wildlife racket? You know, it must take a lot of nerve to do what you've got to do."

106

Chapter 13

The Wildlife Racket: John's Story

John thought for several moments. Then he replied, "Well, I'll tell you that this is indeed a racket, I'll guarantee you that! Everything is so unpredictable. For instance, you never know when you're going to get involved in a poaching situation or, if you do, how it is going to turn out, or what you'll have to go through before it's over.

"I remember well when I started working with the Wildlife Department," he said.

"After a few days on the job, my brother Carl asked me, 'John, why are you at this wildlife racket? I'll tell you something now, my son! You'll never see a moose population in Roddickton. Never!'

"'Well, Carl, boy,' I said, 'only time will tell that.'

"Carl had a reason for making that remark. I remember a time when everything was being killed. I had been working for years with the Foresty Department, and I spent a lot of time going through the woods. I saw what was happening. Everything coming

107

across Soufflets River was being shot. At that time, a moose in the St. Anthony area was a rare thing. In fact, the moose population was as low as it could be.

"Gideon Coles and Bert Lavers were working with the Wildlife Department, but they had no equipment to work with. It was impossible for them to do the job they wanted to do.

"I remember a fellow who was in charge at Corner Brook. 'Look,' he said to the boys, 'as soon as they get all the moose and caribou on the Northern Peninsula killed, the better it'll be! We'll be rid of all of the worry about it then, and it'll be less work for all of us!'

"What an attitude for someone who's in charge to have! No wonder there was so much poaching being done. I'll tell you a good story about it, Joe."

"The first time I got involved in a poaching situation was before I started working with Wildlife. It happened on my first trip to Cat Cove.

"In late April, I thought about making a trip into the high country. I went with Walt Pinsent, the R.C.M.P. officer in charge at Roddickton, and Gideon Coles, the wildlife officer there at the time. I was a Forest Ranger with the Department of Mines and Resources.

"'Come on, boys,' I said. 'Lets go up in the high country.'

"We decided to go by snowmobile to Cat Cove. We got up early the next morning and prepared everything for the trip. Then we started off.

"There was a heavy crust, as hard as flint, making the going excellent. Walt was using the old Sno Jet that the Mounties had in Roddickton at the time, and he was new to the country in our area.

"But there was no problem concerning the trail because a road had been beaten down there. There were so many fellows from Englee and Roddickton in there poaching that all you had to do was to get on their trail and go right as far as Blue Skirt, not far from Cat Cove. That's where they had their cabins; you could say it was the headquarters for their poaching trips.

"We went up over Fly Oil Hill, in over Big Pond, up Johnson's Flats, and crossed Dung Hill. We didn't see any moose or caribou tracks in the area, because almost everything had been wiped out. We went toward the Blue Skirt, reaching the area in the evening. We decided to stay there in Bob Gillard's camp for the night.

"We got up the next morning at the crack of dawn, and got ready to leave. The snow was still as hard as flint. You couldn't see any tracks left by the skis unless you had a pretty good eye. We went on up, keeping just outside Tom's Knob.

"Just before we got there, our eyes suddenly caught sight of some tracks in a little skirt of woods outside Tom's Knob, apparently made the evening before. We could see they were made by a snowmobile that must have been heavily loaded, to have left tracks on the hard crust; the machine seemed to have been dragging the bars. We followed the tracks back to where they had come from—toward Williamsport.

"We went up on the Knob, and there we saw the paunches of I don't know how many caribou. There were two men involved here—one on a sleigh, and the second on Ski-doo. From what we saw, we figured they had killed the caribou, taken out the paunches, cut off the heads and legs, quartered the meat and packed it on the sleigh. I would say they had at least six caribou on it. What an awful slaughter they had made!

"'Now, brother,' one of us said, 'that's it! We've just got to go after them.'

"We left on their trail, hoping to catch up with them.

"If I had been working with Wildlife then, I probably would have been out around that evening after we reached the cabin. Then we would have caught these men right in the act. But it doesn't do any good to think about that now. All we could do was to go after them.

"We got on their trail, headed toward Pelley's Skirt, then Cloud River. We had excellent travelling conditions, and the sun was just starting to rise over the hills.

"I was in the lead, Walt was behind me, and Gideon brought up the rear. I had my eyes glued to the trail, going along by Pelley's Skirt. Suddenly, a flash caught my eye. I stopped and walked back.

"'Boys!' I said. 'I just saw a flash of something!'

"I found out it was the reflection of the sun on the track, and it was made by the wear-bars of the Ski-doo skis. The sleigh being towed behind smoothed the track and made it glassy; the sun shining on it made it really glisten. I looked closer.

"'Look!' I said. 'These are fresh tracks.'

"The fellows looked at them.

"'You're right about that, brother!' Gideon said.

"'Well,' I said, 'this is what we'll do now. Pinsent, you stay on this track. Don't leave it for anything! Just stay on it while we go to check this out.'

"Gideon and I got on the tracks of the two snowmobiles. A little way ahead, we found out how the men had been hunting. They were going around every skirt of woods there. Each time, one fellow had gotten off his machine and walked out through one skirt of woods, probably hoping to drive out any animals that might be there. We continued tracking them for awhile.

"'Gideon!' I said as I stopped. 'We can't be thinking right. We left Walt back there on his own, and he's a stranger here. He's never been on this open country before in his life. If he happens to get astray up here, we'll never find him because it would be awfully difficult tracking him on this hard crust. Nobody knows where he's liable to go. Gideon, ol' man, the best thing for you to do is to go back and get Walt, because these are the tracks of the fellows we're going to catch! They're hunting, and we're on their track. They're not very far ahead of us now, and it's only a matter of continuing 'til we catch them.'

"Gideon turned around and went back to find Walt. The two of them could then catch up with me.

"It was still early, about six in the morning, and the sun was just above the horizon. I crossed George's Lake, went up on the other side, tipped down over the bank, and who should I meet but a man on a snowmobile!

"There was another fellow on a sleigh behind him, sitting on a large cow moose. They had knocked her down, paunched her, cut off her legs and head and placed her side-on on the komatik. They were moving as large as life.

"Popping over the hill, they saw me. The man on the Ski-doo jammed on the brakes.

"'Fellows!' I said. 'What are you doing?'

"'Aw, nothing,' they said in unison.

"'Doing nothing, eh?' I asked. 'You consider this nothing? Well, boys, listen here! I'm working with

Forestry myself, but there's a wildlife officer gone over that way, and there's a Mountie over there, too.'

"'What?' they exclaimed.

"'Caught, eh?' one of them said.

"'Yes,' I said. 'You are. Now I'll tell you what. I'm going to seize your snowmobile, and I'm also going to seize the moose and your sleigh, too.'

"I asked them where they were from.

"'Bartlett's Harbour,' one of them replied. Bartlett's Harbour is a fishing/lobstering community located on a rocky, shallow inlet on the north shore of St. John Bay on the St. Barbe coast.

"'Is there anyone else with you?' I asked.

"'Yes.'

"I looked out on the bog, and there were two fellows on one snowmobile. I couldn't very well leave the fellows I had caught to go after the ones on the bog. If I did, I knew my captives would run away. I hooked on to their snowmobile, ran a line from mine to theirs, put them ahead of me, and started off.

"Gideon crested the hill; he had been looking for me. He had news from Walt Pinsent.

"While I was taking care of poachers on my end, Walt Pinsent was having quite an experience of his own on the other track."

"Six poachers had come in from Bartlett's Harbour. They had left home either very early in the morning or sometime after midnight. They had put off their gear and tent on the Cloud River. There were four adult men and two young fellows in the group. They had been working on a Canada Works Program, but had decided to take a few days off to get a couple of moose for themselves. That's the way it used to be back then.

After throwing off their gear they decided to split up.

"Two men said to the young ones, 'You two go with the others over to the skirt of woods by George's Lake. The two of us will go up near Pelley's Skirt.'

"Four of them went up there on the tracks we had followed. They doubled up, with the younger men on the Ski-doos.

"The other two men stayed for a short while, then came up. Instead of going toward Pelley's Skirt, they kept to the left a little, went east, then down around a small skirt of woods they saw there. They looked out on the open country, and there was a huge bull moose. Naturally, out went one fellow without delay and knocked that one down.

"As they started to cut the moose's throat, they caught sight of another bull not far away. They went over and knocked that one down, too.

"They came back, stopped their Ski-doo, and saw the three of us coming in their direction. They quickly lay down behind the large bull moose and watched us. They later said they saw us when we stopped and had a long conversation.

"'Look!' one of them said. 'Some more poachers coming.'

"Then they watched as we split up, Gideon and myself going one way, and Walt going on ahead, his eyes glued to the track as he passed along.

"Feeling safe, the two poachers hooked onto the moose, towed him across the track we had made, and into the woods nearby. They went back, hooked onto the other moose and hauled that one in. They started to paunch one of the animals.

"Suddenly, one fellow said, 'Listen!' He walked to the edge of the woods, peering around, only to see Walt coming back on his trail. The other fellow came over and watched him as he got closer and closer.

"'He doesn't look like a poacher! He's sitting up too straight.'

"'What do you mean ?' another man asked.

"'He just doesn't look like a poacher!'

"While they argued, Walt Pinsent drew near. One fellow jumped up, saying in a frightened voice, 'Oh my! Look at the yellow stripes! Sure, that's a Mountie! Look at his yellow stripes!'

"This fellow later told me that when he and his buddy saw the stripes, they made a beeline for the woods, where they had their snowmobiles stashed at the back. They were determined to get away from the Mountie.

"Walt apparently went down to Cloud River, but decided to turn around and come back to see where we were, and find out how we were doing. When he reached the skirt of woods, he saw a streak of blood. When the two fellows had hauled in the two moose with their throats cut, the blood had left a streak on the track.

"Walt stopped and looked at the streak. 'Blood, eh?' he said under his breath.

"He saw where the trail went in through the woods, and he followed it in. When he got in through, he saw the two moose. Then he heard the snowmobiles start up.

"He circled out around, saw an opening and made a dash for it, with the intention of catching the men as they were coming out through it.

"He guessed right. The poachers exited just as he entered, almost colliding with them, they were that close.

"He almost beat the blue Sno Jet to pieces. 'Stop!' he shouted, but the men went on, ignoring him.

"He called again. 'Stop!'

"Still they wouldn't stop, so he tried to open his gun holster. He was trying to keep up with them, using his right hand to grip the throttle and steer his machine, while crosshanded, with his left hand, tried to undo his holster and draw his revolver. He finally succeeded, and stopped the men at gunpoint.

"He ordered them to turn around and follow him, returning to where the moose had fallen. As they arrived, Gideon showed up, coming back to look for Walt.

"'Go for John as fast as you can!' Walt said to Gideon.

"This was the story Gideon had for me when he met me coming with the two poachers and a big cow moose on a sleigh.

"One of the fellows with Walt said, 'It's too bad we got caught! We would have had our three moose.'

"Walt and his captives, along with Gideon and myself and the other two men, went over on Cloud River. The rest of the group of poachers then showed up where they had left their camping gear.

"One of the poachers said, 'After all, what's the world coming to? Can you imagine! A Mountie and a game warden in the country! What's it coming to at all?'

"At that moment, we realized they were going to wipe all wildlife out. Shortly before I started working with Wildlife, there were two years when the season was opened in February. In that period, the country was almost cleaned out completely. Back then, Forestry and Wildlife were one department, and they had free

115

access to a helicopter, planes and plenty of manpower; actually more game wardens than we have now. Still, they couldn't control it all.

"I remember one prime example that proved people were slaughtering animals."

"A fellow from Cat Cove told me he and his buddies had a licence. They were up at Little Cat Cove Brook one morning to hunt. There were numerous moose in that area at the time, and these men knew it. Generally, though, the poaching was done mostly on the caribou on the outside of the hills.

"This fellow told me there were four men in his party. They split up a little distance in from the brook. Two went hunting outside. The other two went farther up the brook where it divided. The fellow who told me this said they decided to boil up. Then they heard the two fellows o the outside starting to shoot.

"They shot several moose, and probably got a couple each. Then they started to drive the remaining moose, and in they came. The fellow who was talking with me said he and his friends hid in the woods when they saw the moose approaching. Sixty animals passed by.

"They started to boil up, and in came their companions, whose shots they had heard, and who already had their moose.

"Suddenly, the four of them heard the roar of Ski-doos. Looking up, they saw eight men coming in the brook. The men's eyeballs were nearly popping.

"'What's got the brook all ploughed up?' They asked.

"'That's moose!' the Cat Cove fellows said.
"'Moose?'

116

"'Yes, moose! We just counted sixty of them coming in here from way outside.'

"'You know, we've got our licence.'

"'Oh,' said one of the Cat Cove men, skeptically, 'you've got your licence, have you?'

"'Yes, we have.'

"They left as fast as they could, up the brook to the herd of moose. Over their mugup, the Cat Cove hunters heard the roar of guns. That evening, there were sixty moose shot down on the brook. It was a terrible slaughter. I was told they killed everything in sight.

"I also heard of three men who took out ninety-six animals that winter. Whether or not this is true, I don't know."

"Joe, when I came to work with the Wildlife Department, there was nothing left, nothing at all! You could hardly find a moose on the country. It has cost the Newfoundland Government an enormous amount of money, using its resources and manpower to bring our moose population up to where it is today.

"If they decide to open the season during the winter again, it'll put us back years and years. Snowmobiles have been a big problem, and what was happening was a perfect example. People have easy access to the moose and caribou herds when they have their snowmobiles. Then there are airplanes and choppers. And you have these private planes that fly in, spotting moose for hunters in the winter.

"It's not as simple as it used to be, as we have different hunting methods to cope with now. We're lucky we've got the moose population built up to what it is today. But as soon as a few moose move in close to town and you know the moose population is coming up a little, you also have these fellows coming in with no regard for anything, with nothing but slaughter on their minds. But you don't, in all common sense, kill these cows this time of the year when they're ready to calf.

"Joe, you know, I had another experience that really upset me."

"One night, at about nine o'clock, I received a call from a man in Cat Cove. 'How are you, John?' he asked.

"'Not bad, boy,' I said. 'Not bad.'

"'John, boy, I'm calling from Cat Cove.'

"'Yeah?'

"'Yes. I wish you were here now, boy. Do you know what they're doing up here this time?'

"I said to myself, *Somebody's been knocking them down.*

"To my caller I said, 'Probably someone's been killing some moose.'

"'Well,' he said, 'if that was all that was to it, if it was only a matter of someone killing some moose! But have a guess at what they've done now. My son, they're after knocking down a great big cow, and she was just calving when they knocked her down!'

"'Oh, is that right?'

"'Yes,' he said. 'John, can't you check on them? They always celebrate after a kill, but the way they're partying now, they must have done something special. They wouldn't celebrate like that after killing a normal moose like they've been doing all year.'

"'Okay, brother. I'll get right on it,' I promised.

"I phoned my supervisor, Clarence Maloney, and told him there was an awful slaughter taking place near Cat Cove. I told him I wanted the helicopter for the next morning.

"'Okay,' Clarence said.

"The next morning, the helicopter arrived and picked me up. We flew in to where my caller had told me the kill had taken place. We saw the crows around, as well as the tracks of the fellows. Then we saw the paunch.

"The pilot and I got out of the helicopter. I can tell you that you have never seen anything like it! It was the same as if you walked into a barn. The calf was fully furred, fully developed in every way. I can't say they had shot the cow before the calf was born, or as she was calving, but I do know the calf should have been born. To look at it would almost make you cry.

"Joe, you wonder why I got involved in this job with the Wildlife Department? Well, the first story I told you was one of the reasons. You see, there was a job to be done, and a big one at that. Since I started with the Wildlife Department about twelve years ago, nobody knows what kind of abuse, what kind of punishment and problems I've had to contend with, but all in all it's been a very interesting and exciting time.

"But there's lots of work yet to be done, if incidents such as I just told you are to be stopped. These fellows really deserve to go to jail, and I appreciate what anyone does to help us convict them. Anyone who can do what these fellows have done is nothing but a criminal. There are three dead cows in there with great big calves almost ready to be born. After all, this is the eighteenth of May, the period when calving takes place.

"Talking about work yet to be done: here we are, having caught the boys, Ryland and Luke, but proving the case against them is something else! We still have a lot of investigating to do, a lot of work to do on this case alone.

"I don't know what the outcome is going to be, but we've got some good evidence. I guarantee you that they'll be charged. It's only a matter of striking the right key to the entire thing, because we've got some good statements from these two women we questioned. What they had to say is going to be very tough on the boys when it all comes out.

"Something that really upsets me about poaching is the pattern used. It's no trouble knowing who's at it. Take, for instance, all these white nylon gloves left by the paunches. One fellow's doing all of the shooting.

"Here's what he does. He knocks down the caribou or the moose, puts on a brand new pair of these white nylon gloves and starts to paunch the animal. When he's finished, he takes them off and throws them right in the paunch. There's a pair of white nylon gloves in every paunch we've come to, so that says it's being done by one person. The question is, who can afford to do the likes of that? Who can really afford that?

"So the pattern's set. The reason he does this is because when he puts on his mittens, there's no moose hair or blood going into them. He's aware of the fact that this is how we catch many fellows. We turn their mittens inside out, and there you have the evidence.

"So there's no trouble to know who's at it. And we're going to catch them! There are just no two ways about it. This is one time they're going to get caught!"

After he finished talking to Joe Hynes, Christian noticed him staring at him, shaking his head slowly.

"Well," Hynes said, "all I can say is that I'd rather for you fellows to have that job than me!"

With that, he busied himself, checking things on his boat as they continued on to Englee.

On the same trip, John learned from Joe's son that he and his girlfriend were the watchers who lived in the house near the power plant. The young man excitedly told John his side of the story.

"My girlfriend and I were watching the boys getting ready to go in to haul out the moose," he said. "We didn't see you when you went to the plant, but after Sy Green left, we saw someone get up from among the oil barrels and go to the plant.

"I said, 'Look! There's someone stealing oil at the plant!' We watched when you had to hurry and hide away again. It sure looked suspicious to us.

"My girlfriend asked, 'Who is it?'

"I said, 'It was so-and-so, stealing oil,' but then we saw you stand up, put your pair of snowshoes under your arm and walk toward us. I saw a patch on your shoulder.

"I said to my girlfriend, 'Hey! That isn't someone stealing oil. That's John Christian!'

"I was so excited, I smacked my hands. 'They're going to get caught!'

"I said to my girlfriend, 'Don't say a word about this!'

"We watched you through the driving rain. It looked really weird!

"'Where do you think he came from on a night like this?' my girlfriend wondered.

"'Can you imagine!' I said. 'Coming out of the country on a night like this! There must be something pretty big going on in there somewhere! It's about time they caught them, but look at the price that man's paying. If only there was some way we could help him.'

"'He's trying to save the poor moose,' my girlfriend said."

Chapter 14

Luke Greene Confesses

The boat docked at Englee, and the officers then left by truck for Roddickton. There, Randy Trask took possession of the moose and brought it to Pasadena, where he cut up the meat and heads. He got the lead slugs and took photographs.

In the meantime, John was also busy. He gathered the rifle, rifle shells, rifle slugs, and also the shotgun and shot shells that he had stored away, and took them to Corporal Terry Legg of the Roddickton Detachment of the R.C.M.P. He forwarded them on to Sergeant Swimm at the Halifax Ballistics Centre.

During August, 1985, they received information that Ryland Gill had killed another moose near Cat Cove. This provided another opportunity for them to find the 30-30 rifle they were looking for. They went to Cat Cove and did a thorough search, but again found nothing.

By September, they still hadn't laid any charges. This was mainly because of the fishing season. To arrange a court date during this period was a waste of time. They had planned their moves carefully up until now, but still didn't have enough evidence to lay a charge against Ryland or Luke that would stick in court. They would be patient. John waited until late November before he went up to Cat Cove to try and obtain good statements from some men there. On their way to the community on the 29th, they saw Ryland, who was on his way by boat to Englee.

They arrived at Cat Cove at 2:00 p.m. John went directly to the hydro plant, but it seemed that there was nobody around. In a few minutes, though, Simon Greene showed up.

"John, how are you?" he asked. He seemed to be unusually nervous.

"I'm fine. How are you?"

"Oh, I'm all right," he answered quickly. John considered Simon Greene to be one of his good friends. However, poaching created a shadow over their friendship, and they were unable to talk as freely as they would have liked.

"I guess you know why I'm here, Simon," he said.

Simon turned and stared out the window. "Yes," he said. "I know why you're here."

"First of all, Simon, I have something to show you."

John opened his briefcase and took out the certificate of the ballistics report they had received from Sergeant Swimm. He pointed out that the report confirmed that the rifle Officer Trask had seized at his house had been used in the killing of moose on May 15, 1985.

"Look, John," he said. "I didn't kill these moose, nor did I have anything to do with killing them."

"Well then," John said, "you give me a statement now, saying you didn't kill them."

"I certainly will."

John cautioned Simon and gave him his rights. "Now, Simon," he said, "before you start, there's something I have to tell you. We're considering laying a charge against you, due to the fact that the rifle used to do the killing was found in your home. You know, Simon, that it doesn't look good for you right now, seeing this is your third time being charged. If you're charged and we get a conviction, we'll be looking to Hydro to take strong measures against you, and you know what that means."

He hung his head. "Yes," he said, "I know."

John then took his statement. By the time Simon was finished, he was shaking.

John asked, "Do you think Luke will give me a statement?"

"Yes," Greene said, "I think he'll tell you whatever you want to know."

"Simon, let me put this away. I don't want to charge you in this case. It's Luke and Ryland who we're after, because they are the ones who killed the moose. However, you're the only one we can charge because you had the rifle in your house. But if they'll give us a statement, telling us the truth about what happened, I won't have to charge you."

"I think Luke will talk," he said.

Simon boarded his three-wheeler and went down the hill to Luke's house. John followed on foot. By the time he reached Luke's house, Simon was standing in the basement door, talking with Luke, and stealing glances toward John. As soon as John arrived, Simon left to go back to the plant.

John entered the door and found Luke sitting on a chair in the middle of his basement. He was lighting a cigarette. He couldn't hide the fact that he was nervous.

"How are you doing, Luke?" John asked.

He looked at the officer with an anxious grin. "Not bad, boy," he said. "Not bad."

John sat down and looked around. There was no floor in the basement. It was a new home, and the basement was still under construction as far as he could see. There was a wood furnace near where they were sitting.

"I guess you know why I'm here," he said bluntly. He realized he was dealing with a person who had a different personality than his father. John's voice had no friendliness in it.

"I have an idea, but I'm not having anything to say to you!"

"Okay," John said. "That's up to you, but I've got something to say to you."

"Yes, what is it?"

He picked his words carefully, and decided to hit him where it hurt. John had sensed from Simon that he and his son Luke were not on good terms.

"Your father gave me enough evidence in his statement to convict you on a big game charge involving the moose kills last spring. The rifle we took from your father's house killed at least one, and maybe two moose. Just that fact alone will make a charge stick for your father.

"But there's something more involved here than just a normal charge, as far as your father is concerned. This will be the third charge laid against him, and what do you think it's going to sound like? Can you imagine the chief operator of the Newfoundland and Labrador Hydro Plant in Cat Cove going to jail for moose hunting in May? We will demand that Hydro take strong measures against your father, Luke. What do you think will happen to your father if this goes ahead?"

Luke dropped his head and paused. "Maybe he'll get fired."

"Who knows what will happen?" John said.

"John, the old man had nothing to do with the shooting of the moose."

"Will you give me a statement telling me who did?"

"No!"

"So, in other words, you don't care about what happens to anyone, do you?"

Luke looked at the door, then at the floor again. "The old man only has two more years. Then he can retire from his job," he said. "If he gets fired, he'll lose everything he's worked for."

Luke thought for a moment, then spoke. "I suppose you can't cut off the hand that feeds you."

"Luke, you must consider your mother."

He looked around his basement, then at his new wood furnace. "Look, John," he said, "everything I have here—my new furnace, the building material I got in the house—Ryland's family business let me have on credit. If I tell the truth about the moose, they could come here and take everything I got. But on the other hand, I don't like what he did in there last spring. Ryland's a maniac! What he did in there to those old cows wasn't right, and I don't agree with that kind of killing."

He lit another cigarette.

"Luke," John replied, "Ryland's going to get off with it again, but I've got something to show you. Your father has already told on him. He said in the

126

cautioned statement that you and Ryland killed the moose." I showed him the statement.

"Didn't you get a statement from the women here last spring?" he asked.

"I got a statement from them, yes. But this is where you fellows are going to get an awful surprise. You can be sure you won't go down as telling on Ryland. You'll only be confirming information we already have."

"No, I've got nothing to say."

"Okay, then. I have something to give you." John opened his briefcase, took out a summons and gave it to him. He also gave him one for his father. "This is for the fifth of December, 1985, at 1:00 p.m."

"John," Luke said, "the old man had nothing to do with this. Nothing."

"Then that's what you will have to prove in court."

Luke took a deep breath. "I don't know what would happen if I did tell on Ryland," he said. There was a tinge of fear in his voice.

"I'll tell you what, Luke. I'll be in Cat Cove all night," John continued. "If you change your mind, you know where to find me." He closed his briefcase and left the basement.

When he stepped out onto the road, he looked up toward the house where the women who had given him the statement earlier lived. The statement did not involve Ryland and Luke at all, but nobody else was aware of that fact.

John used that uncertainty, feeling it could be the psychological edge that would make Luke Greene tell the truth about what had happened in the country. He then went down to the boat for supper. He also received more information about the moose Ryland killed with Carl Manuel on February 5, 1985.

Carl, who worked on the coal boats, was now back home at Buchans, a famous mining town in central Newfoundland.

He was told that Helen Blake, the plant worker who had been living in Ryland Gill's basement, was now living in Millertown. Helen and Carl were the keys to this case. If they could get a statement from either one, they might be able to charge Ryland for the February 5, 1985 moose kill, and use it as a plea bargain for a guilty plea on the charge of killing moose in May, 1985.

Luke didn't show up that night or the next morning, so they returned by boat to Englee. John called Clarence Maloney and briefed him on everything that had happened so far.

Around noon on December 4, 1985, John was back in Englee to serve a summons. Driving through town, he spotted a pickup with Luke Greene in it. He went to the marine centre, where Ryland Gill's longliner was moored. He parked nearby and waited until the pickup carrying Luke returned.

He had a summons for Ryland because he knew his boat would be in Englee on this day. John checked and found that Ryland hadn't come down on this trip, but that Luke and Simon were down for court, which was scheduled for December 5, 1985. He then served the summons for Ryland to the captain of the boat.

When the pickup with Luke in it showed up, John asked him where he was going.

"No place in particular," he answered.

"You might as well spend the day going around with me. It'll help to pass the time for you."

"Good enough."

Luke got in the truck, and they headed to the R.C.M.P. Detachment office at Roddickton, although he had no idea John was headed there. On the way, they exchanged a light chatter. John asked Luke where his father Simon was; he had gone to a friend's house. They talked about the fishing season, along with different things.

Then Luke said, "The old man's down for court."

He waited for John to respond, but he remained silent. John wanted to get Luke into the police station, but in such a way that he wouldn't catch on to what he was trying to do.

Just before arriving at the police station, he said, "I've got to drop in there for a few minutes."

"Okay," he said.

He stopped the truck and got out. "Have you met the boys?" John asked.

"No, I haven't."

"Come in, then, for a minute."

"Yes, I think I will."

John kept his fingers crossed. *Is my plan going to work?* he wondered.

They went to the door, rang the bell, and stepped inside. Constable Harry White was on duty. A sharp and alert young man, he was a capable member of the police force. They went into the main office, where the desks were located. It was probably Luke's first time in a police station.

"Constable White," John said, "I want you to meet a friend of mind. Luke Greene of Cat Cove."

This was the constable's first time meeting Luke, but he knew all about him. "How are you doing, Luke?" he asked.

They shook hands.

"Luke is involved in a moose case that comes up in court tomorrow," John said. "Both he and his father have to appear, and between us, I feel really bad about it because of his poor father, and the effect a conviction could have on him. I've talked with Luke about it."

John paused for a moment, then continued. "Maybe Luke would like to talk with you about it for a moment," he suggested. John felt that the constable, being a Newfoundland bayman, had made Luke feel at ease with him by his accent and actions.

"Sure!" Harry said. "If it's all right with you, Luke."

"Okay, sure. I don't mind."

"Go into Corporal Legg's office," John suggested.

"Yes, sure," the constable said.

"I'll go and make coffee," John said.

"Okay," Harry said, as he shut the office door.

John waited anxiously, unable to relax. He made himself a cup of coffee and sat around. Then he heard Constable White call out, "Hey, John!"

He came out to where John was. "What date was that?" he asked.

"Has he told you anything yet?" John whispered.

"No," he said in a low voice, shaking his head.

"It was the fifteenth of May," John said loudly. "Wasn't it, Luke?"

John walked to the office door.

"Yes," Luke said. "I think it was."

"Do you mind if John comes in, Luke?" White asked.

"No, let him come in."

John stepped inside. Constable White got him a chair and placed it next to Luke. Both of them were facing the Mountie on the other side of the desk. The constable had in front of him a caution statement and a writing pad.

"I was just saying to Luke that if his father gets convicted, he would be in quite a mess. John, what do you say?"

"Well," he said, "we might as well face up to the facts, boys. I can't see how Luke and his father will be able to talk their way out of this situation. Now, we're talking about three moose kills, so you know what's likely to happen. I think we should caution you and give you your rights."

The officers did this as they continued to talk to the young man.

"Here's what I'm prepared to do," John said.

Luke was silent. "Number one, if you'll tell the truth, that is, give me a statement," John said, "I'll go out to Englee right now and tell your father to go on back home on the mail boat. We won't even bring him into court. Number two, if you're convicted, I'll ask the Crown attorney to give you the minimum fine. And number three, whatever the fine is, I'll ask the judge to give you six months to pay it. That's all I can do. I'm going to my limit then."

"That sounds pretty fair to me," Constable White said.

Luke dropped his head. Looking up, he said, "Okay, I'll tell you the truth. I can't see the old man taking a rap for Ryland Gill. On the other hand, Ryland went too far anyway when he killed the moose. I'll give you a statement."

Harry started to write rapidly as John asked the questions. After finishing the statement, Luke said he felt a load lift from his back. He also said he would never poach again. He asked John to drop him off at the local store. John obliged him and then went to Englee, and sent Simon Greene back to Cat Cove, as he had promised to do.

On December 5, 1985, District Court was held at Roddickton. At 1:00 p.m., Luke Greene was called to answer to a charge of killing moose in closed season, in violation of the Wildlife Act of the Statutes of Newfoundland and Labrador. He entered a guilty plea. John Christian gave sworn evidence, and related the events of May 15 to 18, 1985, in the Cat Cove area. Wildlife stressed the point of the killing of unborn calves and the time of year when the slaughter took place.

The judge was stern. John read the statement, a conviction was registered, and Luke was given a $2,000.00 fine or sixty days in jail. He was also prohibited from holding a big game licence for five years.

Ryland Gill was called on two charges of having killed moose in closed season on February 5 and May 15, 1985. He didn't show up in court. His defense had called the R.C.M.P. and entered a plea of not guilty on both charges. The time of his trial was set for 1:00 p.m. on February 6, 1986.

Chapter 15

Ryland Gill:
A Man's A Man for A' That

After New Year's Day, Clarence Maloney and
John Christian did a review of the two cases
they had against Ryland Gill. They knew that if
Luke Greene's statement was contested in court and a
voir dire was held, the statement might not be allowed
to be entered as evidence on some technicality in their
case against him for February 5, 1985. All they had
was hearsay evidence, and the defense would certainly
tear this apart. They had to have more. For them to go
to Cat Cove and try to obtain anything else, they knew
would be useless, so they decided to contact Helen
Blake and Carl Manuel.

They began their investigation immediately by
locating both of them. Helen was at her mother's house
in Grand Falls, and Carl was at his home in Buchans.
John left his home at Roddickton and picked up
Clarence at Deer Lake. They drove to Grand Falls and
went to see Helen.

Miss Blake would not give John a statement until she talked with Carl, but she agreed with them that Ryland Gill's poaching had to be stopped. "Mr. Christian," she said, "he has gone too far with it."

She told him enough to make John certain that it would make Ryland scared, after it was related to him by phone.

Carl Manuel finally arrived. He wouldn't give a statement in writing, but he provided enough information to get Ryland in deep trouble. The officers knew that the moment they left, Carl and Helen would phone Cat Cove and report what was going on.

They told Carl about the statement Luke Greene had given them, and how they had implicated Ryland in the May 15, 1985 kill, but that they wanted to nail him for the February 5 killing, too. Giving the appearance of being satisfied, they left.

They knew that when all of the information was given to Ryland, he would pass it on to his lawyer. They also knew that they would then be in a position for a plea bargain.

They returned home to wait. A couple of weeks later, the plan worked. Ryland would be willing to plead guilty of killing moose on May 15 if they withdrew the February 5 charge. Of course, they jumped at the chance.

On February 6, 1986, Ryland Gill was called in court at Roddickton. The charge of killing big game—namely, moose—in closed season on May 15, 1985 was read, and he changed his plea from not guilty to guilty. It was explained to the judge that Wildlife intended to withdraw the other big game charge. When this was agreed to, they proceeded with his case.

This was an important case, so the courtroom and the hallways were filled. Ryland Gill was represented by counsel. Government had Michael Roche, the Chief Crown Attorney for Western Newfoundland, handling the case. John Christian was called to the stand to give sworn evidence. He was amazed at how far the defence let him go in describing the horror and terrible mess of the three kills and the unborn calves. When he read the statement given by Luke Greene, he used words like "slaughter" and "the killing area." Finally, the defense spoke up and called a halt to the proceedings.

The judge registered a conviction in the case. The defense started to plead for his client. He referred to the fact that Ryland's father, a hard-working man, was sick. Secondly, he stated that if Ryland went to jail, the entire town would be in complete disaster because they operated the local snowmobile parts and repair shop. This was an exaggeration, because even the children in Cat Cove could repair a snowmobile!

"It's obvious," the judge said, "that the moose killings weren't done for food. They were senseless slaughter and, for this reason, I fine you four thousand dollars or three months and no licence for five years."

This was the highest fine ever given for a moose violation in the province of Newfoundland and Labrador up to that time.

After the trial, John Christian phoned Clarence Maloney and told him what had happened. They both agreed it had involved a lot of hard, physical work and tons of paperwork; however, they hoped it would serve as a deterrent to poaching in the Cat Cove area.

In the afternoon of the day, after the courtwork was finished, Ryland Gill came to John's home in Roddickton.

"John," he said, "my case is over, and what's done is done. We can't change anything. I came to tell you that you'll never catch me again, for the simple reason that I'll never poach again. I've learned my lesson."

"Ryland," John said, "I am glad to hear that. You're lucky you didn't have to go to jail!"

"I know."

"Ryland, there's only one thing about this that makes me feel bad. Your parents have been very good to me over the years. Now, how can I ever look them in the face again, especially your mother, who has treated me as well as her own?"

Ryland looked at the officer. "John, listen," he said, "you've got your job to do, so keep on doing it. Don't let this stop you from going to visit the old man and mother. Anytime you're in Cat Cove, look us up."

Staring Ryland squarely in the eyes, John thought of the words of the poet, Robert Burns (1759-96). *For a' that, and a' that, a man's a man for a' that.*

Epilogue

During the first week of September, there is a caribou hunt on the Grey Islands. The hunt involves the residents between Cat Cove and Main Brook.

Ralph Randell, John Christian's chief Cat Cove supporter in his anti-poaching efforts, had applied for a licence in 1985. In September, he was successful in having his name drawn for a caribou licence for either sex, to be killed on the Grey Islands. His wife, Lillian, said he jumped for joy when he opened the letter informing him of his success.

Early on Monday morning he left for the Islands, accompanied by his close friend and neighbour, Samuel Brenton, a local businessman, and a fisherman named Gus Young.

John Christian was also on the Grey Islands, conducting the caribou hunt, working with hunters all day. Many caribou were killed during the day. At 3:00 p.m. he decided to go out to his cabin, using a three-wheeler motor bike.

At the edge of the hills he met Ralph, Samuel and Gus on their way in to go hunting. They chatted for a few minutes, and then he turned his three-wheeler around to accompany them. The party had two licences, one each for Ralph and Gus.

They went to a place called Soldier Flats, where Gus shot and killed a large doe. Ralph said that, if possible, he wanted a large stag for a trophy. The four started off hunting again.

They saw more caribou, but there was no large stag among them. Because it was getting late, they decided to go back to the harbour, arriving there at dark. The crew from Cat Cove stayed aboard their boat.

John's son Baine had a caribou licence, so he joined his father while he supervised the hunt. His other son, Norman, stayed behind at the camp. John was accompanied by Bill Roberts, an excellent Newfoundlander and the Habitat Biologist for New-foundland.

Wildlife Technician Ray Sparkes was also helping to control the hunt, along with Fred Patey, the Labrador supervisor with Newfoundland Telephone, who was on holiday at the time. Fred was assisting as a volunteer helper. In fact, it was almost impossible to conduct the hunt without him because he was such an important part of the team.

Early in the morning, Baine joined Ralph and his hunting party from Cat Cove, and went in over the hills in a westerly direction from the cabin. John decided not to join them right away; they could carry on without him. Ralph and Baine each had a licence to fill.

At 8:00 a.m., John left the cabin and headed to the area where the boys had gone hunting. He climbed the hills and started across the flats on top, reaching a height of eight hundred feet or so above sea level, keeping a sharp eye out for the four hunters. He walked for almost an hour, but saw nothing.

He had started to walk up a bog, when suddenly, he heard a rifle shot. It came from a ridge about a mile ahead. He grabbed his binoculars and looked in the direction of the sound, and spotted the group of hunters walking toward him. He started in their direction, stopping at the edge of Shepherd's Bog, where the hunters caught up to him. They began relating their hunting story about a huge stag they had shot on a large bog.

Seeing the stag, they fired at it right away, knocking it to the ground. They ran up to the animal and checked it to make sure it was dead. They put down their rifles and packsacks, and began to get their knives ready.

Suddenly, the caribou jumped up and dashed away. What a surprised group of men! They were in such a panic that they were unable to get another shot at it in order to bring it down again. The caribou ran across the bog and entered the woods. The hunters followed the animal for hours, but didn't get a glimpse of it after.

They stopped for a brief rest near a small pond. Baine told his father later that while they were there, they saw a rainbow. One end of it seemed to be in the pond, and the other seemed to touch the ocean.

"Boy!" Gus Young said as he pointed to the rainbow. "Will you look at that?"

"Yes, we can see it," someone said. "What about it?"

"Well," Gus said, "the old people many years ago used to say that if you saw a rainbow with one end in fresh water and the other end in salt water, someone is going to die before the day is finished!"

"Don't you believe that!" Ralph Randell interjected. "That's an old granny's wrinkle!"

"I don't know much about it," Gus said, "but that's what they used to say."

"Look, my son!" Ralph continued. "There are millions of people dying every day. Rainbows don't have a thing to do with it either!" Ralph appeared convinced.

On the bog, they talked about where they should hunt next. Out of the corner of his eye, John saw the antlers of a large stag on a hill near them, looming against the skyline.

"Look, boys!" he said. "Just look over there!"

The men turned and looked in the direction in which he was pointing. "Look at that!" they said in one voice.

"Boys," John said, "who wants that one?"

"I do," Ralph said.

"Okay then," John said. "He's all yours."

They looked over the area. "Don't move around," he said. "If you do, he might get a glimpse of us."

He continued. "Now, there are two ways to get to him. One way is to go straight up through the tucks, which is hard going for about a quarter of a mile. The other way is up through the valley. It's a mile and a half up there. You can walk all the way in a caribou road. Ralph, pick your choice as to which way you'd rather go."

Ralph paused momentarily, looking at the animal. "I think I'll go straight up the ridge through the tucks."

"Okay," John said, "but you'll have to take your time and be very quiet."

"Yes, I will," he promised. "Sam, are you coming with me?"

"Okay," Sam answered. Samuel Brenton was a soft-spoken person, and everyone enjoyed sitting down and chatting with him.

Ralph and Sam disappeared into the bush. The rest of them got into the caribou trail and walked away, heading for the same animal. They walked for fifteen minutes, knowing that if the animal was spooked or disturbed in any way, it would come in their direction.

Bang! Bang! Shots rang out.

"They're really shooting!" John said. "Get ready, Baine, just in case the stag comes our way."

Bang! That was the last shot they heard.

Then they saw Ralph and Sam waving madly. They walked over to them and saw they had indeed killed a large stag, and were quite pleased with their success.

They paunched the animal. John cut the cap for mounting. They had lunch: Ralph gave John half of his. Ralph did most of the talking during the meal. He spoke about salmon poaching, how the stocks were being depleted.

After lunch, John cut the caribou into five pieces. The trophy attached to the head made one piece, and the four quarters made up the remainder. Four men carried a quarter each, and John carried the trophy.

Baine and his father went ahead of the others. Because they were used to walking, they could move twice as fast as their companions. A mile ahead, they stopped and waited for the others to catch up.

Ralph came over to the rock where John was resting, and fixed the sling on his packsack. He told John he might drop into Englee on his way in and put the officer's son, Norman, off there. He said he would gladly do this because John and Baine were being so kind to him. John told him that anything he had done for him was not only his duty, but his pleasure.

John lifted the load to his shoulders, crossed the bog and climbed a barren, leaving Ralph and Sam behind.

John, Baine and Gus, in the lead, reached a high mountain and stopped to look for a good way to get down. Gus sat down while Baine and John went to the edge of the hill to survey the slope. Seeing no way to get down, they came back to where Gus was sitting.

"Where are the boys?" he asked. "Are they here yet?"

"No, they're not here yet," Gus replied.

John walked back and climbed a ten-foot rise to get a look at the stragglers. He spotted Sam about four hundred yards away, waving a coat.

"Baine," he said, "put that load of meat down, and take your rifle. I think Sam sees a caribou. Let's go!"

He started back toward Sam. Then a thought struck him. He didn't see Ralph anywhere.

Where is he? he wondered. He stopped and called out to Sam, who by now was a couple of hundred feet away. "Where's Ralph?" he asked.

"John, Ralph's dead!" Sam called back.

Unsure if he had heard him correctly, John called again, "Where's Ralph?"

"Ralph's dead, John."

Sam was kneeling on one knee. John ran to him as fast as he could. The look on his face was something that no person could ever forget. It was indescribable!

"Sam, what are you saying?" he asked in disbelief.

"John," he said as he pointed, "Ralph dropped dead back there just over that little rise. There's not a bit of life left in him."

John ran up the rise and looked at Ralph lying there. He could tell immediately that he was dead, just as Sam had said. He still had his thumb hooked in the strap of the packsack still on his back. John felt his pulse and heart, but there was no life. He took him up in his arms and shook him, but there was no reaction. He looked in his eyes; there was no mistake—he was dead.

"Sam," he said, "he's got a twelve-year-old son. Can you imagine what this will do to him?"

They gathered around the body. John asked if Ralph had been feeling sick during the summer.

"John," he said, "I've never known Ralph to have an ache or pain in his life!"

John walked away and said a silent prayer.

Next, they wrapped Ralph's body in John's nylon clothes and returned slowly to the cabin. He broke the news to the others in the party: Ray Sparkes, Bill Roberts and Fred Patey. They were badly shaken. They left in Ralph's longliner for Englee.

On their way, John asked Sam who handled the undertaking in Cat Cove.

"Ralph always did that."

"Well, who can we get to tell his family in Cat Cove about his death?"

"I don't know. Ralph always delivered bad news to families, too."

At Englee, John Christian called the Roddickton Detachment of the R.C.M.P. and reported the death. The next morning, they went out to the island in helicopter and took the body off the mountain.

When Baine and Gus reached the cabin in the afternoon, they sat on a rock near the water. Gus was very upset.

"Baine," he said. "That rainbow! That rainbow! Why did we have to be out here? Now Ralph's dead. That rainbow!" He turned away and wept.

That afternoon, John wrote his report for the police. It stated that his good friend Ralph Randell had died at the age of thirty-nine.

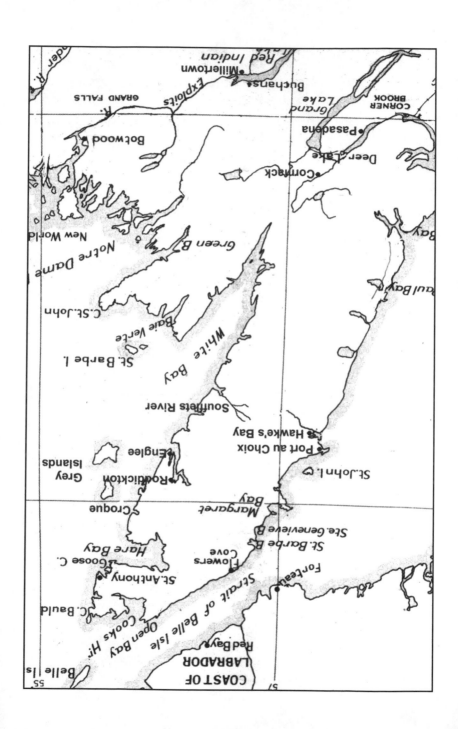